ADVANCE PRAISE

A Path of Oneness is a beautifully guided journey filled with inspiration, awareness and connection. I deeply felt the Divine energy as I read each page. The paradox of each individual's uniqueness from all others while simultaneously being in Oneness with all that there is, is brilliantly expressed. There are many layers to the messages presented which enable all people, at various levels of their awakening, to benefit from the lessons.

— NICOLE MELTZER, SPEAKER AND INTUITIVE
AUTHOR OF *INTUITIVE LANGUAGES*

My mind is blown. This is a beautifully rendered and captivating book. By turns gorgeous, compelling, and surprising, not one of us can afford to miss its urgent message. I pray humanity will be galvanized to come together to face our greatest challenge yet.

— NIKKI D'ANTONI, HEALTH COACH

A Path of Oneness has led me to a deeper understanding of the lessons I've uncovered studying books by Michael Singer, Paul Selig, and Eckhart Tolle. If you are learning to listen to your intuition, access spiritual guidance, connect to a sense of purpose or experience miracles, then this is the book for you.

— JEREMY O'KRAFKA, GRANT WRITER AND
SPIRITUAL SEEKER

A thought-provoking and transformative read! This book will change the way you make every decision in your life. There is a conscious awareness that Ellen brings to the table. No matter your beliefs, there is power in the words on the pages of this book. After reading this book you may realize that you have a choice to live in a state of suffering or a state of abundance and, if you have been living in a place of suffering, you take a deep look at your choices and change how you think, act, and receive. You can transition your focus to living with gratitude and your life will transform. The perspective Ellen offers us of being One is fascinating and will certainly change the choices you make as you interact with others and view the world and the miracles that can and do abound.

— DR. ROBYN REU GRAHAM, AUTHOR OF *YOU, ME, AND ANXIETY*

Ellen Feldman beautifully weaves together her own personal story with her unique insight and wisdom to reveal the truth of Oneness and how this truth expresses itself throughout our lives. Through the experiences of gratitude, miracles, abundance, love, and compassion she shows how we can connect more deeply with this infinite source of being and allow it to complete and fulfill us.

— PHILIP M. BERK, AUTHOR OF *A SINGLE FLOWER* AND *MOUNTAIN'S STILLNESS, RIVER'S WISDOM*

As a channeling researcher, I have been exposed to numerous channeled texts. I'm amazed at the various ways the same deeply inspiring message is delivered by so many different channelers around the world. Everything is interconnected. Growing evidence from scientific fields supports this notion. *A Path of Oneness* embodies the message of interconnectedness in a clear and accessible way, providing guidance for how to incorporate this knowledge in our daily lives and answering universal human questions about our nature and place in the Universe. This timely book is a must-read for anyone wanting to awaken to our interconnectedness and embody that wisdom in service to a better life for themselves and their communities.

— HELANÉ WAHBEH, AUTHOR OF *THE SCIENCE OF CHANNELING*

Reading *A Path of Oneness* was a truly eye-opening experience. The concepts in the book make sense; however, I have not considered them in this way, and I am now reflecting on my life in very different ways. This is a book I imagine I will want to read several times to fully understand and wrap my head around the ideas and truths within. I appreciate that the author(s) had a way of anticipating questions and answering them without me, as the reader, having to even ask. At the same time, I have many new questions as a result of reading *A Path of Oneness*. It is reassuring and inspiring to think of all of the ways we can impact our own lives and destiny, and to know that we are not alone in the journey. For me, *A Path of Oneness* has given new meaning to the phrase "everything happens for a reason."

— LEANNE SHAPIRO, SOCIAL WORKER

If you're feeling unsure about your spiritual path, or just need some reassurance along your journey, be sure to read *A Path of Oneness* by Ellen Feldman. This book will share with you how you are One, devoid of separation from Source and here on this Earth with a divine purpose. Beautifully written, I was at peace as I read this book and at greater peace when I finished it. This book is one I will refer to time and time again. Highly recommended to people on any leg of their spiritual journey!

— JILL CELESTE, MA, AUTHOR OF *LOUD WOMAN: GOODBYE, INNER GOOD GIRL!*

A PATH OF ONENESS

A PATH OF ONENESS

Finding All That Is, Was, and Will Be Inside of You

ELLEN K. FELDMAN

Edited by
DEBORAH KEVIN

A PATH OF ONENESS.
Copyright © 2022 by Ellen K. Feldman

All rights reserved. The contents of this book may not be transmitted or reproduced in any form or by any means, mechanical or electronic, including photocopying, recording or by any information storage and retrieval system, without prior written permission from the author, with the exception only of the inclusion of brief quotations in a review.

Limit of Liability Disclaimer: The contents of this book are intended for information purposes only and may not apply to your individual situation. The author, publisher, and distributor in no way guarantee the accuracy of the contents. The information is subjective and should be treated as such when reviewing the contents. Neither the Publisher nor the author shall be liable for any loss of profit or any other commercial damages resulting from actions taken based on the contents of this guide. All links contained in this book are for information purposes only and are not warranted for content, accuracy, or any other implied or explicit purpose.

ISBN: 978-1-7359333-6-8
Ebook ISBN: 978-1-7372638-3-8
Library of Congress Control Number: 2021949199
Published by Highlander Press
501 W. University Pkwy, Ste. B2
Baltimore, MD 21210

Cover design: Rachel Taylor
Front cover image: francescoch on iStock Photos
Editor: Deborah Kevin, MA
Author's photo credit: Gary Bieler, Definition Photography

CONTENTS

Introduction	xiii
1. How to Use This Book	1
2. An Introduction to Oneness	3
3. The Path of Oneness	7
4. Opening the Door to Abundance	15
5. Reflecting Oneness in Our Relationships	21
6. Miracles from the Perspective of Oneness	31
7. Learning to Talk to God	39
8. Moving Into Gratitude	53
9. Making Sense of Oneness	57
10. The Way Forward	77
11. The Ultimate Message of This Book	87
Epilogue: Final Thoughts	91
About the Author	93
About the Publisher	95

This book is dedicated to
Nathan and Rebecca, my sun and my moon.

INTRODUCTION

When I was little, I did not believe in God. I'm not sure when I became conscious of that, but by the time I was a teenager, it was clear to me that though I felt a connection to the culture and rituals of Judaism that I had grown up with, God was absent from my experience of life. It wasn't until I was twenty years old and my mother was dying of cancer that I turned my thoughts to God in any meaningful way. I was shocked when, months before she died, my mother began talking to me about her own belief in God. I was stunned, actually, when my mother first talked to me about God, something that I couldn't remember her doing at any other point. "What? You believe in God...but, why?"

Her calm assertion that she just did offered me little understanding. Yet, this beguiling discovery created the initial spark of my own relationship with God. On many painful nights in the last months of my mother's life, I looked skyward and spoke to God. "I'm sorry that I don't really believe in you. I need to talk to you now anyway." At the time, my fledgling relationship with the God that I did not believe in enough to truly be a believer, but that I needed enough to allow some seed of belief to germinate, felt awkward. It felt like spiritual puberty. I fumbled and awkwardly bumbled my way through conversations with

God. I cried to and with God. I shared my deepest fears with God and asked God to be with me as I moved through the grieving we do for someone before they die, even as we remain in denial about that eventuality.

Three months after my mother died, I was on a trip to Israel that I had accessed through a lottery that gave away free trips to Israel to young adult Jews. Three weeks before my mother died, I received the news that I had won this trip. I phoned my mother, excited to share the news with her, and she said with a mixture of joy and sadness, "Maybe you could sneak me off to Israel with you in your luggage." When I found myself there just months later, in the very early stages of my grief, I felt my mother with me. I felt her stand next to me and I could swear that I heard her echo in the wind that blew through the Judean desert. In feeling my mother's spirit so clearly with me, I felt God. The experience was so powerful, that I returned to Israel the following year after deciding to graduate a year early from my undergraduate studies. I spent half a year studying in Israel and then traveling across Europe. By this time, my entire perspective had changed. I felt God with me each step of my journey. When things on my journey miraculously fell into place, even in the face of would-be disaster, I credited God. When I faced fear or deep loneliness, I looked to God for help.

Although by my early twenties my relationship with God had already moved from non-existent to a significant force in my life, it would have been unthinkable to me at the time that I would one day write a book about God. There was a lot of pain inside me and for many years, although I believed in God, I did not know how to really hear God. I was a young adult and the mother I had grown up close to was dead. My father, who I had always been estranged from, ended his relationship with me when I was nineteen. I was alone in the world, or so my inner narrative told me at the time. I was blind to this back then, but my early childhood experiences of watching my father abuse my mother and of feeling so deeply unloved and unseen by my father left me with a deep ache to fill what felt like a hole inside me. My father's incapacity to love me had left me with an ingrained subconscious belief that I was unlovable. I dated prolifically, seeking love from a man in a way that I had been unable to receive from my father. I told myself that because I had so little connection to family, it was understandable that I was seeking a partner to build one of my own with. That was understandable, but with a void of self-love inside me, I kept drawing in connections that mirrored my relationship with myself back at me. Men who were initially drawn to me, but who quickly decided that I was "too much," or that they weren't ready for commitment. Men who for one reason or another, could not give me the love that I so badly needed and was convinced had to come not only from someone outside myself but specifically from a man.

I spent years of my life on a quest to find joy and fulfillment that kept eluding me. I went to medical school, convinced that being a doctor would be my true path to helping people. From the minute I arrived at medical school, I felt like an alien from another planet, trying desperately to pretend I was a native that fit in. After two years, I could no longer pretend, and I left for a job in health policy that I had convinced a politician to give me as my stealthily crafted escape route from the path I had been so certain was right for me. From there, I went to law school, not out of a place of wanting to be a lawyer, only in service of my search for joy. Law, it turned out, was not the land somewhere over the rainbow where my joy was hiding. I continued searching, searching, searching for joy in my love life and my professional life.

Eventually, at the end of law school, I decided that it was time to get married. It didn't matter that I had not found a true and deep connection with a man, I had a story, and I was going to make my life fit within that story. I was a young lawyer, and it was time for me to be a wife and mother. I met a man who I was not especially attracted to nor interested in, but somehow, we both got swept up in my story and, less than a year after meeting, were married. We were not really in love, I had just told myself a story that we were because that opened the door to my story of marriage and motherhood unfolding.

This particular man came with his own stories. They were the perfect mirror of my own. They were fabrications, just like mine, that allowed this man's desired story to unfold. Whereas my guiding story was being a wife and mother at all costs, his guiding story was to connect to a woman who would allow him to avoid working. It turned out that my husband had told me a complex tapestry of fabricated stories from the day we met to create the illusion that he had a job and financial resources. He constructed an identity for himself out of stories. At first, I financially supported him while his supposed start-up business got off the ground. Like most pretend businesses, his eventually failed. Over time, he got a more "real" pretend job, but then began the stories to explain why the salary from his pretend job never showed up in our bank account. A series of stories to help the ever-growing stack of elaborate stories make sense. As his stories mounted, mine had to in parallel so that my fragile guiding story could remain intact. Everything was fine! I was married! I was pregnant! We had no money... we had to keep leaving apartments after receiving eviction notices, all of which, my husband explained, were in error because he had most certainly paid the rent in each case. A series of mistakes and misunderstandings on others' part that mirrored the mistakes and misunderstandings at the bank that caused unending problems with his pay being received from his pretend employer.

I had been so clear with God. I was resolute about how my life needed to go. I needed to be married and have children. What I really meant was that I needed to feel loved and connected, but I didn't know how to ask for that at the time. I only knew how to write the story for myself based on my wants, because I didn't know how to identify my needs. God wanted me to feel loved so badly, but I had closed the door to accessing the love available to me, at least during that time in my life.

Things got worse before they got better. We were homeless, squatting on someone's floor with our newborn son and two dogs, struggling to have enough food to eat. I had gone from being a young lawyer with so much promise to someone that I barely recognized. I was completely alienated from friends and family as I worked to conceal the truth of what my life had become. I had gotten everything I had asked God for, at the expense of everything else. I could not see that this was my own creation and that I continually recreated it by asking God to fix the situation so that it aligned with the story that had gotten me into this situation in the first place.

Eventually, something shifted. A miracle happened and I gained access to my husband's emails. I spent hours reading, and on the other side, I was finally able to see beyond the mirage created by our mutual stories. I left the marriage with nothing but a few articles of clothing and my one-year-old son in tow. The day I left was a day of rebirth for me. I sat on the floor of the living room in the small apartment my brother helped me to rent surrounded by the few boxes of things I owned. I had no furniture. No job. No money. I looked at my son crawling happily through his new home and thought, "I have nothing... and I have everything." That new story opened the door to the miracle of where my life went from there and where it is today.

I dated someone new, and two years later, we got married and he adopted my son. We had another child. I had a decent job. A series of miracles had led me from a life that I had perceived as being in tatters, to one that I experienced as being quite beautiful. Yet, something was missing. I didn't know it at the time because I was happier than I had ever been. I just didn't know how happy I could be.

After my second maternity leave, I felt a call within me to leave law and become a therapist. It was a longing that had been inside me for years, but I had never perceived it as a feasible path. Life made the decision easier for me. In the job I was doing at the time, I had had moments of speaking to people in unkind ways that did not reflect how I would want to be spoken to. My boss had addressed this with me before my maternity leave and after my leave, there was no job waiting for me. I was ashamed. I was scared. In those moments of panic when I was forced to face some of my worst fears – that I wasn't a good person, that my worth was in question because I no longer had a job to prove it – I found a deeper connection to myself and God. A miracle led me deeper into myself and God, in fact. I had miraculously told my boss early in my relationship with him that my true dream was to become a therapist. How bizarre, on reflection, that I would ever disclose that to my boss in a legal setting. Yet, I had, and when he fired me years after that disclosure, he reminded me of it. When I immediately began talking to him about where I may find another job in law, he encouraged me to find a path to becoming that thing that sat as a seed inside of me, regardless of how long or seemingly hard it might be to pursue that path.

I may or may not ever have chosen to leave the cocoon of a safe job in law of my own volition. God did not leave it to my volition. God opened the door to that change in a way that left me certain that I was meant to step through it. It was my path, and God was stretching out a hand welcoming me down it. It was not an easy path. It led to conflict with my husband's parents who did not support my decision to return to school. The conflict that my decision sparked ultimately led to a complete estrangement between my husband's parents and the two of us. The stress and pain of the situation sparked depression in me. Not just depression, what I now know how to call a Dark Night of the Soul depression. All of my deepest wounds of abandonment by my father were brought to the surface. I found myself, through an unexpected series of events, at a spiritual therapist, something I had never previously considered. At first, we did deep work to help me heal from the depression. As time went on, our work was no longer about healing. I felt more whole, happier, and more connected to God than I ever had before. I was on a path of spiritual discovery and exploration. My intuition started to expand, and spirituality began playing a more prevalent role in my life. As I finished my Master's degree and began working as a therapist, it felt entirely innate to build my unique approach to therapy on the platform of spiritual belief and outlook that I spent years cultivating with the spiritual therapist. God led me to the place I needed to be in to truly step into my spiritual self.

The estrangement from my in-laws took its toll on my marriage. After years of turmoil between us, it wasn't clear to me that I could stay with my husband any longer. Yet, I did not feel confident in deciding to leave. Once again, God stretched out their hand and invited me on the path that was mine. I went to see a medium and he spent half of the reading telling me that my husband and I are no longer a match and that growing into my true self demanded leaving. I left in shock. Yet, within months, the message I had received was one I could no longer ignore. I left the marriage that had been my safe haven because I felt entirely called to do so, although it seemed like a much less safe path than staying in my marriage.

Almost immediately after leaving my marriage, I experienced a spiritual awakening that changed everything. My intuition had grown significantly, but now I began hearing God talk to me. I heard voices offering me guidance and love inside of me. I began seeing messages, like words and numbers written in my mind. I began having visions of things that would happen. I began seeing clips from past lives like movies inside me. These miraculous experiences grew over time. Months after I began hearing God inside me, I began receiving lessons from my inner guidance. It felt like I was doing a Master's degree inside myself in sacred wisdom. God talked to me about many things. The nature of existence. Love. Trust. Most of all though, God talked to me about Oneness. It was a concept I had vaguely learned of in books that spoke of Buddhist concepts. To be honest, it had never resonated with me. I had seen it as undermining the individuality and wonderful uniqueness of each person. I hadn't understood it all.

Many months after these inner teaching sessions began, I received guidance to begin reading books on Kabbalah. I was stunned. Everything I had been taught inside myself aligned with Kabbalah. I was flooded with gratitude. What made me special enough that God would take the time to teach me Kabbalah?

Any time I asked that or a similar question, God led me back to the same message I received continuously inside myself. "You ARE me, Ellen. You see yourself as distinct from God, but you are God."

Everything that I have received in my life has been in service of Oneness. That is the truth that God has taught me since my spiritual awakening. God has taught me to understand all other lessons from a standpoint of Oneness. The very essence of what moves me to do all that I do in my life is my consciousness of Oneness. My relationship with my children, my partner, and myself is now built on a foundation of Oneness.

God told me that it was time to write a book about Oneness to share this perspective with others. This is the book that God and I wrote together, as One.

I
HOW TO USE THIS BOOK

This book was written as a channelled text. At least, that is the shorthand description for how this book was written that is likely to make sense to the average reader prior to reading this book. What does it mean that this is channelled text? It means that the book was written as a collaborative effort between Ellen Feldman and God. Very often, a channelled text is written with a particular Guide or spiritual entity. Ellen wrote this book with Source.

This book was written as a work that, for the most part, simply flowed through the author. She was called to take time off work and she sat at her computer, and this book simply poured out of her fingers on to her computer keyboard. Parts of the book were a complete surprise to the author, and she continues to reread the book she wrote to glean the full breadth of the guidance God offers through this text.

The pronoun "we" is used to refer to the author throughout the book. Although this pronoun typically refers to the human and divine co-authors, there are times that it simply refers to the divine author.

2
AN INTRODUCTION TO ONENESS

When you look out into the world, it appears as though you are different from the people and natural world around you. In all the ways you can see, you are! Your mother is that person over there living that life, while you're here in this body living this life. The tree cannot speak and is rooted in the forest. You might love it, but it's certainly different from you. Your dog is a beloved member of the family, but he's not you.

By all appearances, you are one of a kind. You are separate from everyone and everything else. The physical world is designed to look this way. Separation between individual beings is what makes life possible. Separation allows for relationships. Relationships (with ourselves, with others, with God, with the world around us) are where life is contained. Without relationships, nothing would happen.

There is a different reality that is beyond what is visible to our eyes: Oneness. The absence of separation. The idea that it is an illusion that we are separate from God, from each other, or from anything in the physical world is a central tenet of Buddhism. This idea reflects the truth that there is one universal energy that animates all life and that is ultimately more than the sum of all the energy that is contained within physical life.

The energy that flows through all that is has many names. In Chinese medicine, it is referred to as chi. In the yogic tradition, it is called prana. This energy is what causes us to experience life coming into our bodies when we wake in the morning. The strength of the flow of this life force into us determines whether we feel invigorated or lethargic.

People often refer to "their" energy. They speak of "negative" and "positive" energy. Energy cannot be possessed. Energy is not mine, nor yours. It does not have particular traits in one circumstance versus another. Energy vibrates at different frequencies. That is what allows color to appear red versus violet. That is why different musical notes can be discerned.

Why does some people's energy feel good to you and others' does not? Why do you feel a shift in the energy of a room when a particular person enters it? The frequency at which the universal energy vibrates when it moves through a particular person at a particular time is determined by a complex set of factors. Their thoughts, their emotions, the stories that they are holding on to in their subconscious. When we feel happy versus sad, the frequency of the universal energy that is moving through us shifts. When we enter a state where we are conscious of the fact that we are energy and that everything around us is energy, our relationship with the energy can shift. A consciousness of the energy that is inside of you allows you to start noticing how you feel as energy moves and shifts inside you. Suddenly, you can notice when energy is moving quickly or when it feels stagnant. The way you feel is affected by how energy is moving through you. When energy is moving quickly, you will feel different than when energy is moving slowly. Energy is always moving through you, even when it feels like energy is "stuck."

It can be life-changing to become conscious of the energy inside of you. When you see life as the movement of energy from one form to another, it becomes easier to conceive of how it can be that you are One with all else in the universe. Energy continuously flows from one form to another. Solar energy becomes kinetic energy becomes potential energy. Left unimpeded, energy moves continuously and seamlessly between forms. When the energy moves into a vessel, it impacts the vessel. Energy can enter you and because it is vibrating at a very high frequency, it may awaken feelings of anxiety, whereas the same energy vibrating at the same frequency may awaken feelings of exhilaration in another person based on their reaction to the energy at that moment.

Why is it important to become aware of the fact that you are animated by the one universal energy that animates everything? This book will explore only some of the answers to that question. All of life is a process of learning the answer.

❦ 3 ❦
THE PATH OF ONENESS

The path of Oneness is one of stepping into your truth. What does that mean? It means living your life in a way that reflects the belief that you are not really separate from anyone or anything. That can appear to be a statement of simply treating other people nicely, in a way that you would want to be treated. We should indeed treat other people as we would want to be treated, but Oneness is more than that idea. Oneness is the idea that you are those other people. You are God. You are the tree. You are the birds in the sky, the land that you walk on, the sun that shines above.

How do we live that way? We start looking at all of life differently.

Why do you have the things you have? Why are you in the relationships you're in? Why have the events of your life unfolded the way they have? Walking a path of Oneness means shifting your answer to these fundamental questions.

When life happens to us, we are a victim of the circumstances in our life. Life is what happens while we watch. The path of Oneness invites us to see life as happening for us, instead of to us. Instead of being a victim to the circumstances that come into our life, we are the recipients of a life path that is meticulously designed to give us what we need. Through our eyes, our path involves suffering. Most people experience suffering at some point in their life, of one form or another. When we refer to getting what we need in life, we do not mean to suggest that anyone needs to suffer. No one needs or deserves to suffer. Experiencing suffering is not inevitable, however. Suffering is a state of mind. A person can experience tremendous growth and even peace through loss or other circumstances that people may automatically associate with suffering. We suffer when our perspective orients us to a story of suffering. "How could they do that to me? How can this be happening to me? Am I always going to be alone like I am now? How can I have messed up so badly?" Those are the words of suffering.

Seeing life as a series of things done for you does not mean not having feelings of sadness. It means that even when we are sad, some part of us can recognize that things are as they are meant to be, even though we are hurting in the moment. The sadness can point us to where we can grow and heal. We can come to know ourselves differently by moving through the sadness that comes up for us in the face of experiences that hurt us. Feeling sad does not mean that we are a victim to the circumstances of our life, it means that we are a human having a human experience. If a person were to lose a loved one and they saw the absence of their loved one as representing loss and loneliness, it is very understandable that they would be sad. Is it inevitable that a person who experiences the death of a loved one will feel sad and lonely? No, it is possible to see a loved one as moving from one state of existence to another and to experience their passing on to the new state with a sense of peace. How do we experience an event that can feel so tragic to one person with a sense of peace? We tell ourselves a different story about what has happened. Telling ourselves that our beloved is gone and we will never do the beautiful things we used to do together again and that that represents a profound loss is likely to result in suffering. Telling ourselves that we have gotten to experience a beautiful thing by experiencing the life of that person and then continuing to experience them in a different form when their soul has left their body is less likely to result in suffering. Sadness and suffering are not the same. Sadness is an emotion, suffering is a state of mind.

You cannot experience Oneness until you make a conscious decision to begin shifting the stories you tell yourself. Why is this step so important to stepping into a mindset of Oneness? Oneness tells us that we are God, and God is us. Being One with God means that we are simultaneously the person moving through the experiences of this life and the God that orchestrates the events of this life. We are the ones that are providing ourselves with this set of experiences! That may awaken a reaction in you of, "No way! I would never give this to myself! I'd give myself all the things that I want! The partner that I want, the job that I want, the house and car and stuff that I want! I would never choose a life for myself that has so much suffering in it."

That is the victim mentality. What does the alternative sound like? It sounds like a story of gratitude. It sounds like a recognition that every moment of life is a miracle. The moments of life that feel good to us are no less a miracle than the moments that feel uncomfortable.

When we shift away from the story of things being done to us and into the story of things being done for us, a new door opens. The door to seeing that everything in your life is as it is meant to be. The way it is meant to be in this moment is not the way it is meant to stay. We are meant to be empowered in our lives. We are meant to set goals and take action and bring about change for ourselves and others. Seeing the way things are as being how they are meant to be does not mean that we are meant to submit to what is in front of us as the best things can be. Far from that, we are meant to be creators in our lives and to steer them in the direction we wish to see them go. Seeing things as being how they are meant to be is really saying that we are not where we are by accident or because of chance. We are there because our life has followed the path it was meant to follow. When we move into seeing life as being where it is meant to be, other options open of where we can move in our perceptions.

"Life is where it is meant to be in this moment," is another way of saying that we know that God has given us exactly what we were meant to receive up to this moment. How does this relate to being One with God? Moving into a place where you are free to perceive your Oneness with God requires accepting that you are the one that has chosen all that you have been given. That is a lot easier to do when you believe that you gave yourself exactly what you were supposed to receive. Consider the alternative. If you've been given an unfair shake in life, and you are God, then God has been unfair. God does not make mistakes. God does not do anything by accident or haphazardly. God is perfection. We may not understand why God has chosen a certain path for us or others or humanity or the planet. Our inability to see the big picture and to discern why things are as they are, why they had to be the way they are, does not mean that the way things are is anything less than perfect.

The only thing you need to know is that you are here. You are alive. You are a miracle just because you exist. There was once only energy. Then God created separation and the endless miracle of life began. Here you are, against all the odds, experiencing things that can only be experienced because you are moving through life with life force energy contained in a physical form.

Where does that leave you? Exactly where you are supposed to be. You are where you are meant to be to have the experience you came into this physical form to have. You came to this life to have an experience that would provide your soul with the collection of experiences that it needs at this time. What is your soul? It is a higher form of energy that moves through a series of experiences, carrying with it memories from across all of its experiences, until it has done everything that it set out to do. The soul is not eternal. The soul moves through a series of experiences, most of which the average person does not recall consciously. People do remember past lives. All people have the capacity to remember past lives, and eventually, everyone will. However, for the most part, the experiences a soul had in previous lives remain beyond the conscious awareness of the person who is currently associated with the soul. The memories from past life experiences guide what the soul chooses to experience in each subsequent life. The tasks and lessons the soul experiences in each life cumulatively guide the soul along its path. When the soul has completed its path, it returns to the universal energy that it was created from. Was the soul ever truly distinct from the universal energy to which it returns? No. Was it ever truly separate from the universal energy from which it was created? No. Yet, it is a distinct entity that moves along a trajectory that is different from the path that other souls made from the same universal energy move along.

Did the soul choose what it would experience in this life? Yes. Did God choose what the soul would experience in this life? Yes. Do you choose what you experience in this life? Yes. They are not contradictions, they are parallel truths.

This all leads us back to the central point in question: Oneness. We can understand ourselves through a story about the person that we are. We can understand ourselves through a story about a higher spiritual reality that remains rooted in separation. Both stories are true and valuable. We can shift to a new story that is based on Oneness. The story of Oneness is not a story of being the same as anyone or anything else. We are all unique and special in our own ways, and Oneness does not efface or deny our uniqueness. Oneness is a fundamental truth about the way the energy that animates different unique beings, both visible and invisible, exists on a higher level. Oneness is the story that explains our reality in a way that makes sense of why things are as they are from a different vantage point.

We already have ways of understanding our reality though, so what does the vantage point of Oneness do for us? Why talk about it, much less adopt it as a way of being in the world?

The truth is that we are One, whether we recognize that to be so or not. Being in a state of recognition of Oneness does not mean learning something new about ourselves. Stepping into Oneness is a path of remembering, rather than learning. You are the same as God. Not like God. Not made in the image of God. You are God. That, whether you are aware or not, is the deepest core truth that underlies every world religion. Yet, you are rarely told explicitly by religions that you are God. Why? What could be the risks of seeing yourself as God?

God is everything and nothing. God is not limited. We often say that God is a purity of love, and that is true. And it is not. God is not love nor hate. God is not good nor bad. God is whatever you choose to experience God to be. If you believe that God demands a certain thing from you and you choose not to do that certain thing, you may experience guilt, shame, or fear. The feelings that you experience in those situations change the vibration of your energy, and that energy shift will awaken a different reality for you. If you believe that God does not exist, you will look out into the world and at your life and you will see evidence to confirm your belief. If you believe God does exist, you will see evidence of God everywhere. The beliefs that you hold and the choices you make based on those beliefs determine the energetic reality that comes to you.

Does that mean that you should not believe in religion? Not at all! Religion is a powerful way of connecting to God and the truth inside of you. Does it mean that religion is made up? Not at all! It means that if religion resonates as true for you, then it is your truth. If it does not resonate as true for you, then find what does. Know that what you choose to see is what becomes reflected back at you. That is not a religious belief, it is an energetic truth.

What does that mean in practical terms? It means that when you open yourself to a path of Oneness, you come to see God everywhere. You are One with God, so you come to see God in yourself. You come to see God in the people around you. You come to see God in the people you like, and the ones you can't stand. You come to see God in the planet. You come to see God in animals, in the natural world, in the water, in everything.

Is this a contradiction from monotheism? No! In fact, Judaism is built on this idea. It may not be discussed as the dominant discourse in the religion, but the religion is founded on the idea of Oneness. A prayer in Judaism that is recited three times per day contains the line, "Hear, Oh Israel, the Lord is God, the Lord is One." This is popularly discussed as being a testament to monotheism, a rejection of there being many Gods, and it is indeed a statement of devotion to one God. On a deeper level though, it is an affirmation of the Oneness of God – our Oneness with God. Mystical Christianity and Islam, like Kabbalistic Judaism, are built on a foundation of belief in Oneness. You can be monotheistic and wholly devoted to serving one God, and step into a belief in Oneness.

What does it mean to step into Oneness when you are a believer in religion? If you are God, what does it mean to pray to God? It means that you are brave enough to step beyond your linear thinking and know that you are simultaneously God and separate from God.

When you step into Oneness with God, you know that what you experience is given to you by you. You are the giver and the receiver. That is the basis for everything else that will be discussed in this book.

4

OPENING THE DOOR TO ABUNDANCE

The truth of Oneness has significant implications for your life. Abundance is commonly held to refer to money and physical affluence. You are right to think that being abundant means having material wealth. You are right to want material wealth. Having more is not a bad thing. Sometimes people who are on a spiritual path adopt the belief that having less connects you more to God. We would challenge that belief. You can have more and be very connected to God. You can have less and be very disconnected from God. What is a problem is believing that material wealth is the path to joy. Joy is not found in things. Joy is not even found in relationships. Joy is a feeling. Feelings come and go. They are like clouds in the sky: when they're there, you can enjoy the experience of them being there, but they necessarily pass through. New clouds come, just as new waves of joy come, but feelings are inherently transient. They are energy, and all energy moves unless some force opposes it.

There is nothing wrong with wanting. Wanting is a part of being human, and your soul chose to come into this life for a human experience. You are not here to transcend your humanity or your feelings that come along with being human. Experience them but experience them from the vantage point of Oneness. When you move into a state of Oneness, you are invited to experience your feelings in a whole different way. There is a path one can walk where one thinks that their feelings are truth. Believing that your feelings are truth is like attaching your life to a helium balloon. The balloon is going to move! It will not provide you with a stable anchor to attach to, just like your feelings. Enjoy the balloon, but do not attach yourself to it, you do not want to be a slave to moving where it moves. You want to be on solid ground.

Does that mean you should ignore what your feelings are telling you? No, there are important messages communicated to you by your feelings. See your feelings as messengers. What is there in your feelings that you can learn from? What do they tell you about you? Stop seeing what your feelings tell you about other people if you want to step into Oneness. We mistakenly believe that our feelings are guideposts telling us how to assess other people. "He's horrible, he's so selfish!" What we really mean when we have a thought like that is, "I feel so angry!" The inward feeling and the outward assessment take us in very different directions. Do you want to attach to the anger in you like a helium balloon? We certainly hope not. You will not like the ride that anger balloon takes you on. Do you want to deny the anger and tell yourself you're above it? We certainly hope not. That anger is energy, and it will move along if you do not oppose it. If, however, you try to avoid the anger and deny it, the oppositional force you are applying to the emotion will cause it to stop its movement through you. Now the energy of the emotion is in you in a different way. Now you've become attached to it, and if you have a story inside you that the energy of the emotion attaches to, you not only need to move through the energy of the emotion itself, you also need to move through the story that the emotion is associated with. Stories attached to emotions in us can live on not only for years in one lifetime, they can follow us across the many lifetimes that a soul traverses. They can move across lineages, being passed from one family member to another, beyond our conscious awareness and knowledge. That is called karma. It is the holding on to a story and an attached emotion.

What does any of this have to do with abundance? It is the basis for our entire discussion about abundance. Karma, at least as we have known it outside of the perspective of Oneness, creates blocks to receiving the amount of abundance available to you in this life. What does it mean to experience karma through the vantage point of Oneness? It means letting go of the idea that karma exists. It means looking at your life and seeing that everything you have ever experienced, including the feelings that have gotten stuck in you attached to victim stories, are what you gave yourself.

When you experience karma outside of the perspective of Oneness, karma is what you carry with you from life to life and from experience to experience in this life because you have a debt that you owe someone. From the perspective of Oneness, that someone that you owe a debt to is you. You wronged your mother, and in so doing, you wronged yourself. How is that any less wrong, wronging yourself? It isn't, as long as we see the things we do as "wrongs." The perspective of Oneness is that everything we do is a part of the master plan that we wrote. The choices you make, the action you take, the things you say. All of it is a part of the symphony of all that is, was, and will be. No note in the master symphony written by God is wrong or bad. You are the human experiencing an endless series of choices in your life, choosing how to behave, and you are also the one who wrote the script of how everything that ever happens will go.

Does that give us license to do whatever we feel like without regard to the consequences? Not at all! It is the opposite. When you are in a consciousness of Oneness, you are more aware of your desire to do right by others because they are you.

Back to abundance. When we are not in a mindset of Oneness, it is easy to move through life guided by our emotional reactions. When we step into Oneness, something else drives us. A belief that everything that happens is exactly what was supposed to happen. When the guiding belief that moves us is that, we have new options that weren't available to us before. We can feel safe knowing that whichever path we take, we will be where we are supposed to be. We can feel secure knowing that if we went a direction that is not in our best interests, we will be guided back the other way. We can rest easy knowing that whichever route we go, if we are open to God's desire to give to us, we will receive what we are meant to have. What we have and what we want may not be the same, but we have what we have because it was what we needed to receive up to that moment. The door to abundance opens when we open. When we open our hearts with gratitude to what is present for us now, we are telling God that the plan as it has unfolded to this point is right and good. That allows God to give more of the plan. The plan is always for abundance. The plan is always for abundance because God could never want to give you anything less than abundance—if that is what you believe God wants to give you.

When you tell yourself a story about what you should have or how unfair it is that you don't already have that thing, you close the door to abundance because you are now a mirror to God showing God that God is unfair. You can tell yourself whatever story you want. What will be will not come from your stories. It will come from what you decided before you came here. Your story about the things you would give yourself if you were God tells you much about what you believe you need. God is not about stories. God is about...nothing. God is not about anything. If we tell ourselves that God is about love, we will find ourselves drawing in love from God. God is energy, and energy is always in flow in the universe. God is the thing you fear most. God is the thing you love most. God is what you tell yourself God is.

Tell yourself stories. We are storytellers. Just do not become attached to the stories. Telling yourself that you want love, connection, money, a partner, or anything else is fine and makes you human. Telling yourself that you need those things or you will not be okay is a different story, with different energetic consequences. You may want those things, but they may or may not be the things your soul/God/you decided to give yourself on your path through this life before you came here.

What you tell yourself is about more than just a story. It is a message to yourself. When you walk a path of Oneness, you come to understand that you are every part of the whole of the created and non-created world. When you come to see that as true, you know that everything you do, think, say, choose impacts the whole. There is no such thing as doing anything without changing the whole universe. Am I speaking of the law of cause and effect? Yes, but I am also speaking of something else, something that is a direct consequence of stepping into Oneness, which is not cause and effect.

You know by now that this book is built on the premise that you are God. If you are God, you want to give to yourself. You don't just want to give to yourself, you want to give yourself an unlimited amount of goodness. You want to fulfill not only your needs but also your wants. The thing is, that you are not just human you. You are the soul that came to this life to complete your tasks and learnings. You are not just the human that you know yourself to be, you are all other humans. You are not just the person you know yourself as, you are the person you know you will be down the road. You are much more than you think you are because you are One with everything and everyone that is, was, and will be. How do you as God give human you the things you want and need while balancing everything that everyone across time and space wants and needs?

Whew. Tall order! Aren't you glad that you don't need to answer that question using your human senses? You would likely hesitate to make those decisions without seeing the bigger picture once you come to understand how big the bigger picture is.

When you come to this life, you come here with certain options open to you. Certain partners, certain career paths. Do you really choose which ones you pursue? Yes, and no. You are the human choosing between one option and another, and no, because you decided before you came here which path you would take. The abundance available to you in this life has already been decided, although you must go through the process of living and decision-making to access it. When it comes to accessing the abundance available to you in this life, you get to decide what to do in the face of the options available to you. You can be grateful for everything that comes to you and be in a state of abundance, or you can be dissatisfied with what comes to you and be in a state of lack. When you are in a state of lack, you are acting as a mirror to God of lack and lack is what you will find in God. When you are in a state of gratitude, you are acting as a mirror to God of abundance, and abundance is what you will find in God. Is that the law of attraction? Yes, it is. There is no way around the law of attraction since everything is energy. It is more helpful to think of this in terms of Oneness though. You are God and God is you. When you choose to be grateful to God, you find yourself in a relationship with yourself that is as it is meant to be. The way things are meant to be is abundant, so being in a relationship with ourselves that is as it is meant to be opens to door to more aspects of the relationship being as they are meant to be because God does not need to work to help you to return to a perspective where you can see that everything is as it is meant to be. That task, of helping people open their eyes to the Oneness that defines their relationship with everything, is what blocks people from accessing the best of what is available to them in life.

You know by now that karma is no longer something you should concern yourself with. Let go of the stories you have carried to this point about what can block you from accessing the abundance available to you in your life. Removing those blocks may or may not mean that the things you have told yourself you need to be joyous will come to you since that was already decided. It does mean, though, that a path of abundance will open to you. It will feel joyous or not depending on the stories you tell yourself about the abundance that arrives for you. You may look at it with gratitude and feel abundant, or you may look at it and feel resentful or angry that you did not receive what you told yourself you deserve. Now you know that looking at your life with gratitude is the key to opening the door to more abundance.

With that in mind, be grateful that you are the one reading this book. You are the one who chose to read it. You are the one who chose to embark on a journey of learning and discovery by buying a book about Oneness. Make sure you remember that you are making decisions every single minute that impact your life. The ones you make today will open or close doors to options down the road.

5
REFLECTING ONENESS IN OUR RELATIONSHIPS

When you come along the path of Oneness, your relationships will inevitably come to reflect this perspective as well. Relationships are your opportunity to experience the miracle of separation. They are where you get to be in a state of being different and unique, while simultaneously receiving the opportunity to remember that you are One with those around you.

What does it mean to relate to others from a place of Oneness? Being in Oneness means seeing that you are the other person and that they are you. That is the truth of your relationship with others whether you choose to see that or not. When you look at others and you see them as separate from you, the way you engage with them will always be limited by the fact that you are denying the deepest truth of your relationship with them.

The wonderful thing about being in Oneness is that you always have choice. You can choose to see Oneness or not. Seeing yourself as being One with others is a conscious choice. Being One with others is not. That is your truth whether you choose to see it or not. When we open our eyes to seeing and living in accordance with that truth, miracles begin to unfold in our relationships.

Miracles? Actual miracles? How so?

Miracles are the gifts we give ourselves to help ourselves to remember that we are One with God. Miracles include fantastic things that happen that are unexpected to us, such as winning the lottery or receiving just the thing we needed in a way that we did not expect. Miracles are more than those things, however. Miracles are the things that happen against the odds of them happening. The energy that began as simply the entirety of what was became, against all the odds, the Universe and everything in it, in addition to what is beyond the Universe. You are a miracle. The very fact of your existence is a miracle. The fact that you not only exist but also live in a body that moves and talks about anything it wants is a miracle. When you move into Oneness, you come to see your life as the miracle that it is. You open yourself to the idea that just being here in this life is a gift that you gave yourself for which you feel grateful.

When that becomes your perspective, you naturally come to see other people and your connection to them differently. You come to see that their very existence is a miracle too. You start to appreciate the fact that since you are One with God, so are they. Since everything that you do, say, and choose was decided by God before you came here, the same is true of other people.

What does that mean in practical terms? It means that when your partner is driving you crazy because they are not doing the thing that you want them to do so badly, that is no accident. That certainly isn't the result of their being flawed. They are God! God is perfect. You and the person you are engaging with in a way that feels uncomfortable are both perfect because you are both God. You can choose not to see them (or you) as God, of course, but choosing not to see that does not make it any less true. The benefits of adopting this perspective are life-changing.

When we come to see everyone around us as God, it plants a seed deep inside of us that tells us that the things people do are what they chose to have happen before they came to this life. The things they chose to have happen are not different from the things you chose to have happen, since you are One. Your process of choosing and their process of choosing was not different. You may want to read that again because it may be a different way of thinking than you're accustomed to. You and the person that you hate most in this world both chose to experience the things that you share in this world. You chose those experiences because they were what your souls needed in this life. On a higher level, all that has ever and will ever happen was chosen by God because every single thing that happens interconnects in a way that allows for the perfect story of existence to play out. The things that you love and the things that hurt you and the things that seem unfair and the things that are what you would call miracles are all what God chose, what your soul chose, what every soul chose, what everything and everybody chose. The fact that you experience those events that unfold in your life that you chose as though you had no role in choosing them is a miracle.

You can see that this book is different from other books. It does not tell you that you should be grateful because of what God gave you. It says that you should be grateful because of what you gave you. It does not say that you should be grateful for the blessings you receive. It says you should be grateful every minute of your life because every minute that you are alive is a miracle.

How does this relate to our relationships? The fact that you are alive is miracle enough. The fact that others are alive with you is another miracle. The fact that you get to interact with each other and go through all the experiences that unfold as a result of those relationships is another miracle. Every relationship you have ever had is a miracle. The ones that you have that you associate with feelings of joy are no more of a miracle than the ones that you associate with feelings of anger or pain. The feelings you experience when you are in or think about a relationship are not set in stone. Feelings change, remember? They are like helium balloons. We do not want to attach to the feelings because they will take us on a ride instead of anchoring us in our truth. What is our anchor? That we are One with everyone who has ever and will ever exist. When you move into this perspective, you know that the miracle is not in how a person makes you feel; rather, the miracle is that there is an experience that you get to have because you are alive and so are they and there is some form of relationship between you.

The beautiful thing about this is that you are going to start seeing miracles everywhere when you adopt this perspective. Your entire day is filled with miracles! You waking up is a miracle. You being able to get out of bed is a miracle. You being alive at the same time that other people are alive is a miracle. It is a miracle when your children say good morning. It is a miracle when your children do something that makes you smile. It is a miracle when they do something that makes you mad. It is a miracle because the entirety of your experience as a human is a miracle. The whole experience is a miracle and you know that you are both the giver and the receiver of the miracle.

When you interact with someone who you associate with feelings that you are uncomfortable with, whether that is someone that you know, or a political figure, or some group of people you have never met, you can know that you are One with them. The feelings inside of you are there because you chose to experience them. The things the people you associate with uncomfortable feelings chose to do the things you are angry about because you chose to have those things happen. You chose the whole situation! You do not consciously remember choosing those things, but you not remembering does not make it less true. Perhaps the only thing you are conscious of is that you get to choose what to do in the face of the uncomfortable feelings. You can choose to act based on those feelings, but that would mean that you are attaching to the helium balloon. You can choose to ignore the feelings and stuff them down inside of you, but that would mean that you're attaching to the feelings and the victim story associated with them. Instead, you can choose to feel the feelings and know that it is a miracle that you are here, on Earth, alive, engaging in a relationship with yourself and others, experiencing discomfort. Every part of that experience is a miracle.

The miracle is not that you can get through the feelings to experience the situation differently. That is a miracle, but so is the fact that the uncomfortable feelings were there for you to experience in the first place. You do not need to attach any story to the feelings. They are just there for you to experience. You may tell yourself a story about everything that the people you associate with the uncomfortable feelings did to make you feel those feelings. They did not make you feel anything. They simply did the things that you chose before you both came to this life. They were simply doing their part of what you chose, and you did yours by having reactive uncomfortable feelings. You get to choose what comes next from your end since that is the part that, from your human perspective, is in your control. From a place of Oneness, you know that on a different level, you are not really in control of that either because you chose that outcome too before you came here, but that is not how you experience the situation.

When you adopt this new perspective, you start to see how different it can feel when people do things *for* you instead of *to* you. People do not realize how often they tell themselves a victim story. "She made me feel so angry. How dare she!" or, "You have no right to treat me that way. I deserve better than that!" The new perspective of Oneness does not ever mean that you should remain in a relationship that is abusive or not right for you. Far from! You should always steer your life in the direction that is most compatible with self-love. Doing so is not only consistent with Oneness, it is necessary. If you do not show yourself love, you are showing yourself that you are not One with others because they deserve love and you do not. Or, even worse, they also do not deserve love! We are all meant to act in ways that are loving to ourselves, God, and others because that means we are acting as mirrors of love to one another. That creates an energetic reality of love. The energetic vibration of love is where all of us want and need to be.

However, you should know that you are not the only one who needs love. The people who you do not like, or that you downright hate, need love as much as you do. They deserve love as much as you do. How can they not, they are you. When you step into Oneness, you come to see that when you direct anger or hate at someone, you are really only directing it at yourself. Then there is an energetic reality of anger or hate that we all experience since our energy is really one universal energy. You raise the vibration of the one universal energy every time you choose to experience love and you lower it every time you choose to experience anger or hate. Does that mean you should pretend you never feel angry? You know by now that the answer is no because doing so would only cause you to become attached to the anger and to the victim story you associate with the anger. Telling yourself that you are not allowed to feel anger is just as much a victim story as any other. When anger arises, feel it, and know that it will pass through just like the clouds in the sky. You do not need to release anything; the anger will just move along like all other energy if you do not apply an oppositional force to it or become attached to it.

When you feel anger, though, the perspective of Oneness reminds you to consider the messages that the feeling is sending you. All feelings are messages that you chose before you came here to send yourself at particular moments. If you do not receive the message, the message will need to be sent again in a similar or different way. You are not likely to want to receive that message again, it would probably feel most comfortable for you to receive the message the first time. In all likelihood, the message is related to the story you are telling yourself. You may not even realize that you are telling yourself a story of any kind. We are storytellers by nature and you tell yourself an endless stream of stories to guide you through life. "I'm hungry, maybe I'll eat," is a story. "The sky is full of clouds, I think it's supposed to rain," is another story.

You rarely go long without telling yourself a story of some kind. The goal is not to stop telling stories; you are not designed to do that. The goal, if you are trying to walk a path of Oneness, is to start shifting your stories from victim stories to Oneness stories. Oneness stories are always about you, never about other people. All the other people in the whole world are really just you. It is an illusion that they are different from you. They are only here on Earth with you to give you an experience. If you spend your time looking out at them, trying to figure them out, or, worse, judging them, then you are missing out on your own experience. Your experience is why you came here to live a human life, so you are missing out on the miracle of your life!

Get over the idea that it is ever helpful to judge someone else. When you adopt Oneness, you know that judging them only means you are judging yourself. Judging yourself is a painful experience. No one enjoys being judged, it makes us feel like we are not good enough, like we are not lovable. We all want and need love and when we feel like we are not good enough or not lovable, we experience pain. Pain lowers our energetic vibration and then draws in more experiences that in turn lower our vibration further. We need experiences that raise our vibration and in turn raise our vibration further.

From the standpoint of Oneness, you have everything you need to live a perfect life right now. You may not have the things you have told yourself you want, but you do have the ability to perceive your life as a miracle regardless of its circumstances. If your life is a miracle, then regardless of what else is true in this exact moment, you are a manifestation of God's plan. You can rest easy knowing that when you see yourself and your life in that way, you are opening the door to all of the abundance that God has in store for you, that you chose for yourself before coming to this life. You can open yourself to the goodness planned for you regardless of how much pain you are in because doing so does not require you to be joyous. You can be in deep pain and still be grateful. You can be in sadness and still know that your life is a miracle and that it is unfolding according to God's plan.

What does this have to do with relationships? If your life is unfolding according to God's plan, then all the things you experience in the context of relationships are also unfolding according to God's plan. When your partner cheats on you, that was a part of the plan. When your best friend stops talking to you, that was a part of the plan. Your plan! When you experience any painful situation, you can know that everything is as it is meant to be and be grateful for the miraculous experience of having this situation unfold, even as you move through the feelings that are uncomfortable for you. Does that mean that you should avoid relationships to avoid the pain that comes with them? That would mean missing out on the miracle of being alive along with other people who are also alive.

Be aware that being in a relationship is not a one-sided affair. Other people are also living out the miracle of experiencing all the things they receive from you. Although it is true that they are God and they chose what they would experience in this life before they came here, including the uncomfortable parts, you are here to experience being human. Part of the human experience involves making choices. You may have decided what you would choose before you came here, but you nonetheless experience the miracle of getting to make choices through the consciousness of a human. You get to choose whether to treat other people as the God that they are, as the reflection of you that they are, or whether to deny the Oneness that unites you. When you treat others as you would want to be treated, you experience a mirror of the way you are treating them reflected back at you. You treat others with love, and love is reflected back. Not necessarily because of how they treat you. They may react with kindness or cruelty. This is an energetic truth we are referring to, which may or may not be mirrored in your immediate experience with another person. You may choose to treat another person with cruelty because that is how you feel they treated you, but all you are doing, if you follow that path, is perpetuating the mirror of an energetic vibration of cruelty. Energy is not cruel nor kind, but the energetic vibration that accompanies cruel behavior is very low and will draw in more energetic experiences of a low vibration. That is not something that you want for yourself.

The path of Oneness never demands that you think of others ahead of yourself. In fact, elevating others ahead of yourself is contrary to the principles of Oneness. No person is more important than any other when you look through the lens of Oneness. God is not more important than you, you are as important as God. It does mean though that you are not more important than anyone or anything else. Your want for things is not more important than the wants of any other person. Your needs are not more important than the needs of the people you are in relationships with. On a very practical level, stepping into Oneness means coming to see that the needs of all people are equally important and that relationships need to be changed to accommodate this truth. We need to rethink how we engage with our partners, our clients, our children, our parents, and, something that can be challenging to conceive of at first, strangers. Moving into Oneness demands relinquishing our stories of blame that we direct at other people. Even when our stories are based on what we consider important values, like justice and equality. Justice and equality are entirely consistent with Oneness, but when we take our story of Oneness and convert it into a story of blame, which is simply a victim story turned outward, we have left the anchor of Oneness that we chose to attach to. Now we are once again attached to the anger helium balloon, somewhere we never want to be. To come back to solid ground, we need to remember that blame is irrelevant in the world of Oneness because we all, as One, chose everything that would ever be done. We can choose to step away from blame and instead experience the miracle of being humans who make empowered choices as the reflections of God that we are. This allows us to move forward in a way that recognizes the equality of everyone's needs.

Does this sound a little like advocacy? It should, because moving onto a life path of Oneness truly is a path of advocacy. Not everyone plays an explicit role as an advocate, but simply by choosing to look at people as being One with you and One with God, you are choosing to advocate for Oneness in this world. Recall that energy is universal, so whether you raise the universal energy's vibration through advocacy work or by making choices in your personal life, you are inherently advocating for a world that is more aligned with the vibration of love.

The path of Oneness is not an idea. It is an energetic reality whether we choose to ever experience it consciously or not. It is also a miraculous opportunity to shift our relationships in a way that allows us to experience them as more loving, more considerate, more harmonious, and more equitable. We are not referring to relationships simply as the ones we share with the people in our lives. We have a relationship with ourselves, with God, with the planet, with the spirit world, with all that ever was and all that will be. You can shift your relationship with everything and everyone to come to reflect the values of Oneness. You want to receive all the things you want and need in this life. The more you give, the more you are able to receive. That is an energetic reality. The more you give people by seeing yourself in them, the more you receive a mirror of people seeing themselves in you. The more you give reverence to the God in others, the more reverence you will receive in the mirrored experience of people engaging with you. Give others the gift of seeing them through the lens of Oneness and draw in all that you will receive as an energetic result. Again, this is not about what you receive from others in every human exchange, this is about having the courage to take a broader perspective on our life experience. You will know that you are experiencing a reflection of Oneness coming back at you when you start to see miracles in your life. See the miracle of others' existence, exactly as they are. See the miracle of the planet being as it is, exactly as it is. See the miracle of God inside yourself, exactly as you are. When you start to see those miracles, even greater miracles may start to appear in your life.

6
MIRACLES FROM THE PERSPECTIVE OF ONENESS

When we speak of miracles, we are not speaking of the parting of seas or the burning of bushes. We are referring to the things that you do for yourself, from the perspective of Oneness, that give you what you need in an unexpected way. Sometimes you need reassurance that you are not alone. A miracle may look like an old friend calling you at just that moment. Perhaps what you need is guidance on how to make a particular decision. A song may come on the radio that contains a lyric that seems to speak directly to you, providing you with the insight you needed just then. A miracle, from the vantage point of Oneness, is a gift you give yourself to tell yourself that you are God. What does that look like?

It looks like you deciding before you came here that at some point on your journey through your human life, you would start to receive clues to remind you of the truth of who you are. We do not mean the truth of who you are as the person you consciously know yourself to be. We are referring to who you are from the standpoint of Oneness. The truth that you are God and everything and everyone that is, was, and will be.

How do these miracles start appearing in your life? In an infinite number of ways. Some people start experiencing a deepening of their intuition. Others begin hearing God speak to them. Some people start seeing messages. Miracles that are intended to awaken you to the truth of Oneness can come in the form of seeing repeating numbers, such as seeing 4:44 or 5:55 when you happen to check the time. Miracles can happen in any size, shape, or form. Most frequently, people begin to experience synchronicities in their life. They begin seeing, hearing, or experiencing the same message repeatedly. The same words may be said by different people in a short time frame. The same dream may recur. The same thing may show up in your life over and over, and you may not have any idea why. You may, alternatively, derive your own reason to explain the synchronicity. You may decide that the message was there to hurt you. You may think that it was just your imagination. You may decide that it was cool, but not worth paying attention to. Whatever you do in response to the miracle, you decided before you came here what response you would have, so there is no reason to feel bad or ashamed about how you have reacted to anything in your life.

When you start to become conscious of miracles intended to awaken you to your truth of Oneness, the most amazing thing happens. The more you pay attention to the miracles and recognize the miraculous nature of the events, the more they start to happen. This is, once again, a reflection of the energetic reality of all that is. It is not a reward for noticing the miracles, and it is not a punishment if the miracles stop appearing when you do not pay attention to them, it is simply an energetic truth that the more you sit in a vibration that is associated with the miracles, which is an even higher vibration than love, the more things that vibrate at that same frequency will be drawn to you.

You always want to raise your vibration because of the energetic consequences of doing so. When you raise your vibration, you raise the vibration of the entirety of the universal energy. Does this mean that you will personally draw in more abundance to yourself? Certainly, within the confines of what you decided for yourself before you came to this life. However, you know by now that you are not just you. You are all that is, was, and will be. You may have spent most of your life not recognizing that, but once you start down a path of Oneness, you cannot unknow the fact that when you experience goodness, the vibration of all that is rises, and when someone else experiences goodness, the vibration of all that is rises. When anyone or anything experiences a lowering of their vibration, the universal energy lowers as well. Does that mean that you should descend into shame any time you yell or engage in any act that is likely to lower your vibration? Not at all, you chose to have that experience, but you should know that you have the immediate ability to shift the situation by returning to a perspective of Oneness as soon as you become conscious of the fact that you lowered your vibration.

You will start to see that when you step down the path of Oneness, these miracles that are intended to awaken you to your Oneness start showing up more and more. The floodgates may open, and you may start seeing God everywhere. You may start knowing that God is trying to communicate with you and you may start communicating with God. Very often, people start hearing God give them messages of love, guidance, and Oneness.

Is it a miracle when you hear God speak with you, either indirectly through a message or directly through a voice or knowing or image inside of you? Of course it is. Is it any more of a miracle than the miracle of your very existence? No, not at all. It may appear to your senses that hearing God is more of a miracle than you being alive but that is only because you have become so accustomed to being alive. Eventually, if God speaks to you daily, you will become accustomed to that too. It is not any less of a miracle on the hundredth day that God speaks to you than it was on the first, yet, through your human senses, it may appear that way. Let go of the idea that miracles need to come in the form of things that are outside of your normal sphere of experience.

Start to see miracles in everything. It will likely feel easiest to start to see miracles in the things that you associate with joy, such as watching a sunset or walking through a forest or sharing a laugh with someone you love. Start to expand your awareness though of just how many miracles you can experience in your daily life when you let go of the idea that you must feel joy for something to be a miracle. You can feel sad that you lost a job and witness the miracle of the experience. It is not a miracle because your brain tells you that there is a silver lining in the experience. By all means, find the silver lining, but the miraculousness of the experience does not hinge on the silver lining story that you have told. The miracle of the experience is found in the fact that you are here and this miracle is unfolding, including any other people or things that are also miraculously involved in the experience.

Why is it important to start seeing miracles everywhere in our everyday life to be on a path of Oneness? When you take that step, you open much bigger doors for yourself, and therefore for all that is, was, and will be.

When you start to inhabit a world that is full of miracles, you raise your vibration to a whole new level that is where a different kind of experience becomes possible. You open the door to accessing more of the truth of your Oneness with all that is, was, and will be. You are always One with all that is, was, and will be. Seeing miracles does not create the miracle of Oneness. Raising your vibration sufficiently, however, makes it easier for you to remember that truth on a deeper level. I am not referring to a conscious remembering, I am talking about an energetic remembering. To facilitate the miracle of coming into a physical life form defined by separation, you experience an energetic shift that allows the volume of energy that is contained in your soul to exist in a physical body. The vibration of your soul must be lowered dramatically to be able to exist in physical form. One of the consequences of that lowering is that it becomes significantly harder for you to connect into the various facets of your connection to the Oneness of universal energy contained in other physical and non-physical forms.

You may know people who can tell you what will happen in the future, or who can talk to dead people, or who speak with their Spirit Guides or angels. Are they special and unique because they have these spiritual gifts? Of course they are, just as you are special and unique because of all the ways you are different from every other person who has ever been and will ever be. You may think that they do something that you cannot, and you are right, and wrong. You, like, every other person, have the ability to become attuned to the truth of Oneness in a way that allows you to connect into all other aspects of Oneness.

You have the ability to talk to trees. Yes, trees can communicate with you and you can communicate with them. You have the ability to communicate with animals, with God, with angels, with deceased people, and with all aspects of the visible and non-visible world. Since time is only a construct experienced through the physical plane of existence, all that has ever happened and all that ever will happen is just as much a part of Oneness as what is true at this moment. You have the ability to see and know about your past lives and the past lives of others. You have the ability to know what will happen in the future. Are there limits on your ability to access all these ways of connecting to Oneness? Yes.

You are limited from accessing these gifts by various factors. Since everything is energy, there is an energetic reality of needing to be in a particular place of energetic vibration to connect into the energetic connection to the Oneness. How can that be? If you are One with everyone and everything, why does the frequency of your energetic vibration matter in terms of connecting into that which is truly you? It matters because, as discussed before, you enter the physical world at a lower vibrational frequency that allows for a "forgetting" of the truth of Oneness. The truth of Oneness is true regardless of where your vibrational frequency sits, but the question of whether you remember it is impacted by your energetic reality. Again, we are not talking about conscious remembering, but energetic remembering.

Everyone is intended to awaken to the truth of Oneness at some point. The entire universe is undergoing a continual process of ascension. The ascension process has nothing to do with what a person believes, it is an energetic phenomenon. The vibration of the entire Universe is rising and has been doing so steadily since it was created. Will it ever stop? The frequency of the physical Universe will continue to rise until the physical container that holds the universal energy can no longer contain a vibration of such strength and it ruptures. That will occur in a number of years that cannot be contained in this book. Many universes have come and gone. An elaborate discussion of that is well beyond the scope of this book. Suffice it to say, ascension is not a new phenomenon, although it has been discussed in the spiritual community in recent years in a way it has not been previously.

All people are experiencing the effects of the ascension process, whether they are spiritual or not, whether they believe in God or not, and even whether they believe that everything is energy or not. You are undergoing a process of ascension right now, and you have been since the minute you were conceived. You may know that; you may not. Some people experience symptoms of the ascension process and because of the stories they choose to tell about their life experience, they relate their symptoms to the energetic ascension. Others also experience symptoms of ascension and because of the different stories they tell themselves, they link those symptoms to entirely different root causes. You can tell whichever stories you choose. Why is it important to being on a path of Oneness to be aware of the process of ascension that is being experienced by the entire planet? There is a highly relevant reason that impacts your life.

The process of ascension is not just an energetic reality, it also has implications for the way you access the abundance available to you in this life. Maybe you are wondering how the rising of the frequency of the universal energy impacts your process of accessing abundance. If it is universally rising, shouldn't everyone be experiencing more abundance? It certainly doesn't look to the human eye as though that is what is taking place. What you see with your human eyes and what is true on a deeper level often do not align. Everyone is experiencing a rising of their energetic frequency, but this only opens the door to the possibility of accessing more of the abundance that was allocated to you as available in this life by your soul before you came here.

You want to access all the abundance that you can. Remember that abundance does not mean money or other worldly goods. Abundance means plenty. It means plenty of health and love and connection and joy as much as it does material wealth. Whether you think your life is abundant or not, and we certainly hope you do, there is always room for more abundance. If you are telling yourself a story about having enough abundance, shift the story. That is not to imply that you should tell a story of lack. There is an important difference between believing that you are lacking and being open to receiving more. The story of lack will not help you, an openness to receiving will.

We encourage you to look at all the stories of lack that you currently tell yourself. Get honest with yourself about where you may be telling yourself, consciously or subconsciously, that you have not received what you think would make you happy in life or what you believe would be fair. You do not need to get rid of these stories, you are One with all that is, so where would they go? You just need to start telling yourself different stories. You know how to change the stories you tell; you do it all the time. One day you tell yourself that your partner makes you so angry you could leave them, and the next day you tell yourself that you shouldn't get so angry at your partner. You changed your story. You may think that changing your story about whether you are lacking the money or the job or the partner that you need or want is hard, but you may come to see over time that it is a lot harder to hold on to the story of lack because it feels painful to sit in the energetic vibration of lack.

When you shift away from your stories of lack to stories of gratitude for all that is here in your life right now, you open the door to being more open to receive. You may think you are open to receive now because you will gladly take all the abundance anyone can give you, but that story that you are telling yourself about your openness to receive has little to do with your energetic openness to receive. Energetic openness to receive is about sitting in an energetic frequency that communicates on a vibrational level that you are One with all that is, was, and will be. Do you need to believe in the idea of Oneness to be in that vibration? No, not at all, but it helps.

When you walk a path of opening your eyes to the truth of Oneness, you inherently lift the vibrational frequency that you are in. When you do that, you tell God that you are God. When you tell God that you are God, then God knows that you are receiving the miracles that were chosen for you to awaken you to the truth of Oneness. Since you are receiving the miracles, more miracles can be sent because of the law of energetic attraction. When more miracles are sent, the miracles bring abundance into your life. The miracle of abundance, once again, does not necessarily mean that you will receive money. The miracle of abundance means that there is more goodness brought into your life. Is it a forgone conclusion that you will look at the "more" sent to you and experience it as a miracle, or even as a positive thing? No, it depends on what story you tell about what you receive. If you see the miracle that is sent to you and receive it with gratitude, then the law of attraction draws more miracles to you. More miracles coming to you means that the vibration of your energetic field rises, which in turn creates an even stronger energetic pull for miracles.

By seeing the miracles in your life and receiving them with gratitude, you are setting yourself up in a cycle of positive reinforcement to keep drawing in more abundance into your life. By experiencing this cycle through a lens of Oneness, you experience the added benefit of knowing that you are the one giving yourself the miracles. Why is that important? What that means is that you are both the giver and the receiver. When you are both the giver and the receiver, you raise your energetic vibration even higher. Why? Because being the giver means that you are tapping into the creative energy inside of you. We can use the name Source Energy for the frequency associated with that vibration. Source Energy is a very high-frequency vibration. Once you tap into that, a whole new set of benefits opens to you. That is will be the subject of the next chapter.

≈ 7 ≈
LEARNING TO TALK TO GOD

The whole premise of this book is that you are God, so what does it mean to learn to talk to God when you are God yourself? The point of stepping into Oneness is not to convince yourself that you are all that there is. You are here in this world surrounded by billions of other people. You are the only one who is quite like you. You are not alone in the visible world. You are surrounded by angels and ancestral guides and spirit guides and many other types of celestial beings who are with you throughout your life to help you on your journey. You are One with all of them. Being One with them does not mean that you cannot be in a relationship with them at the same time. You are One with your partner, but you still have a relationship with them. It is the same with God. You can simultaneously be One with God and have a relationship with God.

You can have a relationship with God without talking to God. There is a very good reason to talk to God though. When you talk to God, God talks back. Some people hear the voice of God talk back to them. Other people receive a knowing inside of themselves or images that are communicated from God. Still other people hear God through the miracles that come to them that we discussed before.

God seeks to talk to you. God wants to be in a relationship with you.

Wait, you mean that the universal energy that was described as not being anything but rather only a reflection of what we see in it wants to be in a relationship with us? What does that look like?

When we talk about God wanting to be in a relationship with you, what that means is that there is an aspect of the universal energy that is given the job of helping you to remember who you really are. The aspect of the universal energy that has the job of guiding you back to your truth of Oneness is what you might call God. There is much more than that to the entirety of the universal energy. The entirety of the universal energy is what is all that is, was, and will be. That is what is referred to as God in the dominant discourse in Judaism. We will not go into detail here, but there is another aspect to God that is beyond energy, that exists beyond existence. That is right, there is something beyond energy even though everything is energy. What is beyond energy cannot be described in words or conceived of by humans, it is only described as nothingness in Kabbalistic Judaism. That is all that will be said about that in this discussion. It is simply relevant to understand that there is no one thing that "God" refers to. You may think of God as being the loving parent who reaches out to you to support you and guide you through difficult times. You may think of God as the energy that is everything and everyone that has ever been and will ever be. You may think of God as being more than any of that. You may think of God as being something that you learned from a religion that does not resonate with any of that.

For the purpose of this discussion, we are referring to the loving and guiding parent who is here to help you along your life path and beyond. That understanding of God is what we refer to any time we refer to God in this book other than when we say that God is not love nor hate, not good nor bad. God is more than a loving parent who guides you, and God is exactly that at the same time, just as you are the human that you know yourself to be and more than that at the same time.

When we refer to talking to God, we mean to say that there is an option available to you to tap into guidance and love in a way that you may not have experienced before. You may have a knowing inside of you that God loves you. We hope you do, whatever that means to you. When we refer to speaking with God, we are not referring to the prayers that you say, whatever those look like. Please pray, by all means, if doing so makes you feel connected to God or any other way that feels good for you. We are referring to something else altogether though.

By talking to God, we mean that you have the ability to receive guidance that will help you to reach the potential your soul came into this life with. There is a certain amount of abundance allotted to each soul in each life. You do not know what the abundance is or will be, only what you get. You do not ever miss out on abundance because what you receive in your life is exactly what you were always going to receive. Does that mean that you could not have received more? Yes, and no. Yes, because your path was never going to unfold any differently, your soul decided before it came here exactly what would happen in your life. No, because that is not your experience of life as a human. Your experience is that you are making every decision and choice and that these decisions and choices dictate where your life will end up. On a level, they most certainly do! If you do not act as the creator and driver in your life, you will not go anywhere. If you sit and tell yourself that God will provide for you so you do not need to act or choose or do, it is unlikely that your life will yield very much other than a lot of sitting.

When you come along the path of Oneness, you start to see that none of the ideology of Oneness in any way detracts from your motivation to work hard and strive to improve your life. Your life is in your hands. You get to decide what you do with it. It is true from the standpoint of Oneness that the path is already determined, but the determined path assumes that you are going to do the work and make the choices and drive your life in the direction that you ultimately do.

Well, then if the path is already determined, what does it mean to say that a certain amount of abundance is allocated to you in each life? It means that although the path is already known and certain, your experience of it does not reflect that and as you move through life and navigate the various choices available to you, certain doors open and others close. If you choose a particular line of work instead of others, the doors you chose not to walk through close. If you choose to live in a particular city versus another, the person you will meet and marry and have children with will be different, meaning that the doors you could have walked through in another city will close.

It may be certain which doors you will walk through and which will close, yet there is a parallel truth that you have to decide which ones will be yours. You know by now that walking a path of Oneness demands surrendering your need to apply linear thinking to what you hear. You can choose any of the options available to you. Not every option in the whole world is open to you. It may be nice to tell yourself it is, but it isn't. You were born in a certain country to certain parents. You cannot choose to have different birth parents or to have been born in a different country. You cannot choose to marry someone who already chose to marry someone else unless they choose to leave that someone. You cannot choose to be the birth parent of the child someone else gave birth to. There are particular paths open to you. There are many, many, many different paths open to you—a staggering number of paths if it were communicated in human terms—but the choices are finite.

Accessing guidance to lead you along your path in the way that best serves you is a vital tool to help you access the greatest amount of abundance along your path. We will remind you again that abundance does not refer only to material wealth, but rather all the plenty that you could ever want and experience in your life. You want to access all the abundance available to you. It is what you came to this life for.

Being on your path means that it is perfect, regardless of the direction it goes. It means that there is no such thing as a wrong decision. You cannot redo the things that are already done. If this discussion awakens pain or guilt or any other painful emotion, stop and think about what story you may be holding on to about how your life should have gone. You are exactly where you are meant to be. You were never going to be anywhere other than where you are at this exact moment. This exact moment is perfect, as is your path.

This moment is a place you want to be. Being in the past is not compatible with Oneness. The past is gone, it does not exist. Although we have memories and those are treasures to us, living in them is not being alive. There is no place where the memory exists, it is just a story. Stories change, as you know by now. So do memories. Abundance cannot exist in the past. It is only something that has relevance in the present moment. You cannot give yourself abundance in the past, only now. You are God, and you want to give yourself abundance.

If human you is so busy looking back at the past that they are not here in the moment, you cannot give them all of the abundance that is available to them. Not because you are mad at them and want to teach them a lesson. Not because you think that they need to be taught how to be in the present moment. It is an energetic reality. If you are living in the past, you are not here in the moment. If you are not here in the moment, your energy is not focused in this moment either. If your energy is not focused here, then you are not open to receive abundance in the way you would be if you were here. The past is gone. Tell yourself that everything you have ever received on your path was exactly what you were meant to receive. Then put the past away with gratitude and come to the present moment.

Any time you catch yourself wondering if you took the right turns on the winding path of life, remind yourself of this and come right back to the present moment. It doesn't matter how long you spent away from the present moment, as soon as you realize that you're not there, you just bring yourself right back. It's as simple as that. Know that every human wanders away from the present moment, that is normal. It is just as easy as bringing yourself back.

How does all of this relate to talking to God to receive guidance to help you on your path? Being in Oneness means that you know that you are God, so put yourself in God's shoes. If someone is present in the moment and wants to talk to you, you will want to talk to them more. If you are not present in the moment, you are sending a message to yourself that you are not interested in being here and talking. That does not mean you are being judged. It just means that you want to talk more when the listener is ready to listen. You want to talk to God. Trust me, the guidance available to help you access the abundance available to you will help you immensely on your path.

Why is all of this so important? You may never have spoken to God and you seem to be doing just fine.

Good question. You may think you have never talked to God. You may never have heard God speak with you. You may not even believe in God. You have received a lot of guidance on your path from the moment you were born whether you realize it or not. You have been guided every second since you came out of the womb. You have heard this guidance. Some of it sounds like the voice in your head. Some of what you hear in your head is powerful guidance, in fact. Some of what you hear in your head is not though. Some of what you hear in your head is distraction. Some of what you hear in your head actually steers you away from the path that would result in the greatest amount of abundance for you.

How are you supposed to know what is guidance and what isn't? How are you supposed to navigate all of what is going on in your head?

You aren't. Listening to your thoughts is not advisable. Your thoughts can take you on an even wilder ride than the anger helium balloon we talked about earlier. Attaching to your thoughts is inadvisable. You will be led on a path that has no stable footing. Why is that? Because like feelings, thoughts are like clouds. They move. They change. They are energy that passes through you and you do not want to attach to them. Unlike feelings though, thoughts are even lower vibrational forms of energy. They cannot be trusted. Does that mean that you should be at war with your thoughts? Should you be trying to stop the thoughts from coming?

Absolutely not. Trying to do that will actually cause you to attach to them. The thoughts are there for a reason. You do not have to listen to them. That is the change that everyone in existence should make immediately. Your thoughts are not truth. Just because you heard something inside of you does not make it true. Your thoughts are what you have that grounds you in this world. They give you something to keep you from floating back up to the spirit world. They are of such a low vibration that they give your soul a low vibrational hook to hold on to.

As we discussed before, the laws of energy cannot be circumvented, they only exist in ways you may not be used to when it comes to the spiritual world. Your soul vibrates at such a high frequency that anchoring it in the physical world is a miracle of epic proportions. It is not obvious that it should even be possible, yet it has been happening for billions of years. Yes, billions. Humans are far from the first species in which souls have incarnated. That is not the discussion that is relevant to this book, but it is being said to try to shake you out of the stories to which you may have become attached. You are far from alone in this universe, you just lack the capacity to see what other life is all around you.

Back to the thoughts and why they are so important. The thoughts are an energetic weight that keeps your soul anchored. You may never have heard about this energetic explanation for thoughts. The fact that it is novel to you does not make it any less true. The fact that there are other stories that can be told about thoughts and why they exist does not negate this story. You already know that stories can be true in parallel without any one story detracting from the truth of the other.

Thoughts are there for energetic reasons. They cannot be avoided, nor should they. Why are we not talking about the subconscious and what you can learn from your thoughts? Why are we not going into a mindfulness-based discussion about thoughts? Why aren't we discussing your ego, superego, and id? Because the path of Oneness can co-exist with all of those ideas, but it does discourage you from attaching to them. The path of Oneness is rooted in energetic truth. Why is that beneficial? Because those other approaches, while valuable and relevant, are still rooted in separation. The path of Oneness always brings you back to your Oneness with all that is, was, and will be. Your thoughts are not something separate from you. They are a part of you. They are not your truth. They are not you. They do not define you, they do not even give you very much valuable information about you. They are there for an important reason, however, even if that reason may not be something you think about often. The fact that you never thought about energy or the energetic value of your thoughts does not mean that you need them any less than you do. Let's be clear: you need your thoughts. Not only would it not work to eliminate them, but it would also mean your soul could not remain anchored in your body if you succeeded in doing that impossible thing.

What does all of this have to do with receiving guidance from God? You cannot trust your thoughts, those low-vibrational transient bursts of energy that move through you nearly constantly. You cannot trust your feelings either, we hate to tell you. Although they are higher vibrational to your thoughts, they are still transient like thoughts. What can you trust?

Intuition. Intuition is that knowing inside of you that sometimes causes you to just know that something is a certain way. You have certainly experienced it. Some people have a more robust relationship with their intuition than others because their soul decided before coming here that that would be the life experience of the person they are entering in this life. That says little about the person or even the soul, it truly only says something about the path the soul chose to take in this life. The path is what determines how the person will act, look, and behave in this life. You may think that your soul has the same characteristics as the person you believe you are. It is accurate that each soul is unique, no two souls that have ever existed have ever been the same, just like people. However, the relationship between the uniqueness of your soul and the uniqueness of your person is rarely the same.

You may think that when you enter each life, the person that you are is similar to the last one, just with a different appearance. That could not be less true. You may think that you are smart and that you must therefore have been smart in past lives. That could be true, but there is no reason to assume that based on the stories you tell yourself about how you are in this life. You are not a collection of characteristics. Those things that you believe to be true about yourself are just stories. Stories change all the time. If stories change all the time even in the same life, they certainly do not remain the same between different lives, or across the thousands of years that most souls travel between different lives. The lives that a soul lives are determined based on what tasks and lessons are given to the soul. The soul may need to learn by being in a life where it has the option of choosing whether to steal or commit murder. The soul may need to learn from coming into a life where it hears God with ease from birth, or where it is raised Buddhist, or where it has the option of becoming a drug addict. None of those choices are given to the soul because it is good or bad or has this or that characteristic. It all has to do with the path the soul has chosen to take before coming to each life, all of which ultimately fits into the much bigger picture of all of the souls' paths determined by the God of all that is, was, and will be. All the souls' trajectories fit into a master plan of the story of everything.

That may be a lot of new information. What about that is important for you to know? You are here for a reason. You are here to live out a journey that you chose before coming here. You are the way you are on purpose. It is not an accident that you may be what you call stubborn or lazy. Does that mean that you should just tell yourself that you are the way your soul chose you to be and that there is nothing you can or should do about it? Not even close. The fact that you chose to come into this life inclined to act a certain way does not mean that you should passively remain that way. You have given yourself an opportunity to choose to act in different ways. You are not good or bad because of the way you currently act, and you will not be better or worse based on any changes you make to the way you act. You cannot be good or bad, you are just energy at the end of the day, and energy is neither good nor bad. However, you can choose to act in ways that reflect the fact that you are One with all that is. When you treat others in ways that reflect your Oneness with them, you step more fully on to your path of awakening to your truth. Regardless of the specific tasks your soul came to this life to fulfill, your soul is always in each life with the goal of awakening to the truth of Oneness. Why? Because that raises the vibration of the universal energy and that is the goal of every soul that has ever existed. Raising the universal energy brings all that is, was, and will be to a higher state. That is the ultimate purpose of all of existence.

When you enter the world as a soul, you rarely remember your purpose in coming here. That is different from the tasks you are here to complete. Your purpose is the very essence of why your soul chose the path it did. Tasks get completed as part of the journey through life, but the purpose is the root of why the path is chosen. Everything in your life is built around completing your purpose in life.

If a soul's purpose is so important, why don't we know what the purpose is? If you knew your purpose, you would focus exclusively on the purpose. The miracle of being would be lost. Being in the world without knowing your purpose is done for you, not to you. There is no reason to be focused on your purpose. If you are in Oneness, then you know that every step of your path is perfect regardless of which choices you make because you have given yourself everything you received along your path. You may not be conscious of this truth, but it is nonetheless true.

When you come back to the path of Oneness, you know that parallel but non-contradicting truths are the name of the game. On the one hand, your path is perfect regardless of which way your path goes. On the other hand, your path can be smoother and more efficient if you receive guidance to help you along the way. You are being guided whether you realize it or not, but receiving more guidance is always what you want. You will be guided whether you listen to the guidance you receive or not, but it becomes easier for more guidance to flow to you if you listen because of the law of attraction. Not because anyone's feelings are hurt if you do not listen, only because of an energetic reality. You listen to your partner and they will want to share more with you, you listen less and they will want to share less. That sounds like an emotional reaction, doesn't it? It may be with your human partner, but it isn't with God.

With God, the relationship is dictated by the laws of energy. You may feel very loved by God, and you should, the message here is not to conceive of your relationship with God in sterile or non-loving terms. Please do give and receive love in your relationship with God, that is a part of the miracle of being in relationship, and you do not want to miss out on that miracle. The message is, rather, that regardless of the love in the relationship, the relationship nonetheless conforms to the laws of energy. Listen more, more guidance is drawn in. Listen less, less guidance is drawn in. You may think that listening means that you have to do the thing you are told to do. That is not the case. Listening means being open to receiving, not following orders. You are never, ever expected by God to make the decision that aligns with what you are guided to do. Your decision is yours to make. Listening and obedience are not the same thing. Seen from the lens of Oneness, you make your decisions in a place in your head that is influenced by many factors. Each one of those factors is a part of the Oneness that is God. You do not make your decision independent of God, you are making it in the very place that is God—you! You can choose to know that or not, but it's still the case.

When you were a baby, you came to this life and you were perfect. You opened your eyes after emerging from the womb and you did not know a single thing about yourself. You felt the urge of needs—the need to eat, drink, be held, be comforted. You did not know how to get those needs met other than by crying. Over time, you learned how to recognize your needs and to communicate about them in other ways. You felt like you were doing a good job doing so. You weren't. That may sound like a surprising thing to read. You were not doing a good job communicating your needs.

Why would we say that? Why would we even deem to know that when we've never met you? You know what? We have. We are God. We have met you. You have not been doing a good job communicating your needs. You have not communicated with us in a way that we are able to hear you.

How can we hear you? When you do not ask for things. When you communicate to us that you know that you have what you need, we hear that there is a green light for us to continue to give you the abundance we have allocated for you. When you come to us and tell us that you are lacking and you know what you need, we hear that we have not done a good enough job giving you what you need.

That may upset you to read. We think it might. Maybe you think that is us saying that you should not pray. Maybe you think that that is a message that you should not share your pain, your wants, your desires with God.

No. That is not the intended message. Please share all your feelings with us. We are seeking to have a relationship with you. A close relationship must be one where you can feel safe to share your feelings. If you are sad, mad, scared, or any other uncomfortable feelings, we want to hear it. You have wants. That makes you human. Share your wants. You want to change your life, as you should! We do not want you to feel that life is as good as it can be, because it isn't. It can and should be better, no matter how good it is. We always want to make it better for you.

Then what are we saying? We are saying that while you are busy telling us that you are scared and want to change the things that make you scared, while you are telling us that you are mad and want help to change the things that make you mad, tell us that you are also grateful for what you have. Tell us that you also know that the way things are now, as much as they need to be changed, are also the way they are meant to be. Do you have to say that? No, that is not a formula for manifesting the things you want to receive in your life. There is no magic combination of words for you to use to convince us to give you the things you want. We want to give you the things you want. We are constantly trying to do so, within the bounds of what is possible in light of what your soul decided before you came to this life. The problem is that the way you have been communicating your needs to us to this point has created unintended energetic barriers to us doing so. Everything is energy and conforms to the laws of energy, even if the laws of energy are applied in a way that may not be predictable based on human expectations.

When you tell us that we are doing a bad job giving you what you want and need because things are not as they should be—that is not your intention in the way you are speaking, but it is the consequence—you are saying that you are not open to believing that this is the way things are meant to be. That creates an energetic effect. You may not realize it, but that creates the effect of you being less energetically receptive to the abundance that was always intended for you. Why? Because you signaled that the way things are, which is the plan, is wrong. The energetic vibration of wrongness is very low and that means that you are no longer in the vibration that makes it possible to continue to provide you with the abundance that was planned for you. You must see by now that the laws of energy have nothing to do with whether you are loved or not and nothing to do with what you deserve. That is not to say that we think you deserve any less because you communicate in a certain way. Not at all! There is no one way to communicate and this book is not intended to create a uniformity of communication. Communicate in your style that reflects who you are, your values, your religion. You are you, and who you are is perfect. Who you are is who you decided you would be before you came to this life.

When you communicate in a way that signals that the plan as it is unfolding is wrong, the plan typically needs to be adjusted to reflect this message. That does not mean that the plan as it has unfolded is wrong or bad. It is exactly what it was always going to be. You know that you are where you are meant to be if you are there. When you open your eyes in the morning, that is where you are meant to be. When you look at the people you are surrounded by, they are where you are meant to be. When you look at the job you are in or the lack thereof, that is where you are meant to be. Are you meant to remain there? Goodness, no! You are meant to move to a better place in your life continuously.

All the abundance available to you is sitting in the cards waiting to be accessed. This is about how to access it in the most efficient way possible. The most efficient way to access the abundance available to you is to adopt an attitude of gratitude. Sounds cliché, right? It isn't. An attitude of gratitude is your way of saying that everything is as it is meant to be.

You may be asking yourself how you can possibly be expected to be grateful when your life is so awful! That is exactly what we are talking about when we say that you are doing a bad job communicating in a way that makes it possible for us to give you the abundance available to you. You are being inundated with beliefs about your abundance. You are continuously hearing from society that you need more, that you deserve more, that more is better. We actually agree, but not in the way that you think. More is better but not when it comes from a place of believing you are currently lacking. More is better when you believe that you are currently abundant. The law of attraction makes that an energetic reality. The morality of it has nothing to do with this book. We are making a case for the energetic reality of Oneness. There are other ways of experiencing these same ideas. This is the focus of this book.

The energetic reality of Oneness is such that when you believe that you are lacking, you vibrate in a place of lack. When you vibrate in a place of lack, you know that you are not where you are meant to be. When that happens, abundance cannot flow to you as easily. Not that it will not flow to you, but there are barriers to it flowing in the way it might have otherwise.

The best way to overcome this problem is to see that there is no problem. It doesn't matter where you have been or how you have been thinking and speaking. The moment you change the way you are speaking or acting, the energetic vibration inside of you changes. It is never too late to change. All you have to do is make the change!

What we are saying is this: talk to us. Tell us how you feel and what you want and what doesn't feel good about your life. We prefer when things feel good, of course, but you are free to feel however you feel. No matter how you feel and no matter what is true in your life right at this moment, you are always able to be grateful. Even in moments of absolute grief, there is room to be grateful. You are able to be grateful no matter what comes along. No matter what you are experiencing, you can be grateful. When you move into gratitude, you can be grateful no matter how you are feeling, and gratitude is the key that will unlock a whole new set of opportunities in your life.

8
MOVING INTO GRATITUDE

When we refer to moving into gratitude, we mean to say that you should adopt a perspective of gratitude that pervades every aspect of your life. You know that being grateful acts as a gateway to abundance. Why? Because gratitude is your way of saying that everything is as it should be. Being as it should be means that abundance can flow to you in accordance with the plan for your life in the most efficient way possible.

What does it mean to move into gratitude? It means seeing everything in your life as being given to you by you. You are the giver and the receiver. That is the basis of Oneness. You are God and you are the human. You are both humans in your human relationships. You are the parent and the child. You are everyone and everything. Have you ever felt you got more from a situation where you gave than when you received? Maybe you have been a volunteer somewhere before and felt like you received more from the people you helped than you gave to them. That is because of Oneness. It has nothing to do with being a nice person. Maybe you think you did something nice for the people you gave to, and you did, but on an energetic level, you gave to yourself. Giving to yourself means that you are simply moving energy between yourself and yourself. The more the energy moves, the greater the flow of energy. The energy is universal. It is not our energy to give nor your energy to receive. The energy is going to flow regardless of whether you give or receive, but when we consciously give and receive, we experience the miracle of being in Oneness while still experiencing separation.

The most beneficial thing we can do to help ourselves is to know that whatever we receive is given to us by ourselves. You know that what you receive from you is what was always meant to come to you because you decided that before you came to this life. The fact that you are here experiencing the unfolding of that plan that you made for yourself is a true miracle. How can we help but feel grateful to be experiencing the unfolding of the miraculous plan we made for ourselves?

The best thing you can do for yourself is to sit back and enjoy the ride through life. How can you do that when life is hard and painful and confusing? By bringing a perspective of gratitude to the whole experience. By bringing gratitude to your life experience, your whole life will change. We promise you! Will you draw in more abundance as a result of the shift in your energy? Yes, you certainly will as an energetic reality. Again, you may be excited by the increased abundance that flows to you or not, that will depend on whether you see what you receive as abundance and whether you tell yourself a story that feels good to you about what you receive. However, the second you shift your perspective to one of gratitude, your life immediately improves without any of the facts about your life changing. Try it. The minute you adopt a perspective of gratitude, your whole being feels different. If you're doing it in a way where you really mean it, you will feel a vibration throughout your body that is different from what you felt before. You will know if you mean it because the vibration cannot be made up. What do we mean by really meaning the gratitude? Gratitude is not about the words, "thank you." Saying "thank you" is nice and can make the people around you feel appreciated. God has no ego and does not need appreciation. Saying "thank you" is helpful if it truly helps you to adopt an actual attitude of gratitude, but you can say "thank you" and lack any actual gratitude inside of you. If gratitude does not mean giving thanks, what does it mean? For the purpose of our discussion, it means stepping into an actual belief in the idea that everything is as it is meant to be. Maybe the words "thank you" help you to feel that way. If they do, by all means, say them. We encourage you to try saying, "All is as it is meant to be," instead. Why? Because doing so is more likely to remind you that that is the essence of what you are trying to say than the alternative.

Gratitude from an energetic perspective is really about bringing you into Oneness. It is about opening yourself to the energetic abundance available to you. It is about reminding yourself continuously that you are the giver and receiver of everything in your life. Do you have to be grateful to receive abundance? Goodness no, everyone receives abundance. Do you have to be grateful to be in a state of Oneness? No, everyone is whether they recognize that or not. Do you have to be in a state of gratitude to open the door to the next level of miracles that are possible in your life? Our answer is yes, and we are inviting you to adopt the same answer for yourself.

9
MAKING SENSE OF ONENESS

Let's begin by reviewing what we know so far about Oneness.

You know that Oneness means that the fact that you are separate from any other person or thing is an illusion. You are the same universal energy as every other person and thing. You can tell yourself whatever story you want about how different you are from the other people around you, you are still subject to the laws of energy, and the laws of energy dictate that you are the same manifestation of energy as them. You have uniqueness, that is true, as do all other people and things. You can tell yourself that your uniqueness means that you are not possibly the same as anyone. Not believing that you are the same is different from not believing that you are energetically One. You are meant to be different from all other people. That is miraculous. If energy is all One, it is a true miracle that no two people have ever been the same. You can tell yourself that that is an accident, a random occurrence, and you are entirely allowed to believe that. You are allowed to believe anything you want. This book is a gift that we are giving to you to help you see things differently, to tell a different story than you may have heard to this point in your life about why things are the way they are. Why? Because seeing things in this different way will open up pathways to making your life better.

When you step into Oneness, you know that there is no distinction between making your life better and making the world better. You are One with the whole world so making your life better means you have improved the world. Does that sound like permission to only care about yourself and what happens to you? It shouldn't. This book means to make the case that when you are One with all that is, was, and will be, you inherently come to realize that just being about yourself means you do not accept that you are truly One with everyone else. If you only care about helping others, you are excluding yourself from the Oneness. You may come to see that having an equal desire to see yourself and every single human experience the maximum amount of abundance available to you is a true manifestation of Oneness.

On a practical level, what does living a path of Oneness look like? It looks like being exactly where you are and knowing that that is where you chose to be. Have faith that you have not made a single wrong turn in your life. You can make a million choices and after one million twists and turns, you will find that you have landed at the only place you were ever going to be because that is the path that you chose for yourself. Make decisions moving forward that reflect this new understanding. You can choose to do what your thoughts and feelings tell you to do. Your thoughts and feelings are both there for a reason—an energetic reason, as well as any of the other reasons that you have learned previously. When you understand your thoughts and feelings from an energetic perspective, it becomes easier to see that they are just energy, and they move and change as energy does continuously. What you feel in this moment may or may not be what you will feel in the next moment. They are important insofar as they will guide you to a certain extent. Beyond that, however, your thoughts and your feelings are not the best guidance available to you. They may be the only guidance you have known how to draw on to this point. You may be saying that you have never only been guided by your thoughts and feelings, you have always drawn on the guidance of other people, like your parents or partner. That is true. Their responses to you are valuable, but they are ultimately mostly guided by their own thoughts and feelings. You have never really only been guided by your thoughts and feelings, or those of others though. It may appear that way, but you have been receiving guidance from God from the minute you were born. You are One with God, you have to know that by now, so whether you believe in God or not, you have been connected to the universal energy that is God because it would be impossible not to be.

There is more guidance available to you. There is more guidance available to everyone. The more we shift our energy to allow for more guidance to come to us, the more guidance will come. The guidance that comes from God has nothing to do with thoughts or feelings. There is a place inside of you where you know the difference. Intuition cannot be described in words. It is a place of knowing that is unlike a different kind of knowing inside of you. Go to that place. Open yourself to a deeper knowing and rest easy in the knowledge that everyone has intuition. That is the place from which most people currently experience their guidance from God. However, as the energetic vibration of all that is, was, and will be rises, an increasing number of people begin to experience communication from God in different ways.

You may begin to hear God speaking to you. If you do, you are not hallucinating, you are not imagining it. It is possible for every human to hear God. It is even possible for every human to experience visions sent by God. It is possible for every human to communicate with any human who has ever been or ever will be, alive or dead, inside of themselves, because you are by your very nature One with them. People awaken to these abilities constantly. They may or may not talk about these abilities, but many people have them and do not even admit it to themselves because society has pathologized being able to speak to God or receive auditory or visual messages from God. It is regularly called mental health disorder to do so. You can tell whatever story you choose about the ability to hear or see God. You already receive a knowing from God in the form of intuition. If you open yourself to communicating with God on a deeper level, you will receive more communication from God. That is not because you will be rewarded by God if you open yourself to talking more, and you are not being punished if you do not. It is an energetic reality.

Are things ever as simple as we might make them sound here? Yes, and no. Energy is extremely simple. It conforms to very basic and easy-to-understand laws. Those laws are immutable. They cannot be circumvented or changed. The way things look to you, however, may or may not look simple. You may tell yourself, for example, that you are very open to talking to God, you are trying and have been your whole life and yet God never talks back. That may make you feel sad, inadequate, unloved, angry, or anything else. If you are open to talking to God and you are not hearing God, there is a reason. You can tell any story about it that you want, but we promise you, there is an energetic reason. You cannot know for sure what the energetic reason is, different energy workers and healers will give you different answers. Some will speak of karma. Some will speak of blocks in your energy. Some will speak of whatever other story they choose to tell based on the guidance that comes to them or their own thoughts and feelings. The bottom line is, when everything is energy, you always have options of how to work with what is right now.

You start by seeing what is right now as what is meant to be. You know that where you are is where you are meant to be. You tell yourself a different story. The minute you change your story, you are well on your way to changing your life. Then you walk through life in a different way. The way of Oneness. You walk through life knowing that you are One with everyone and everything, both visible and invisible. You speak to God. You speak to the loved ones you wish to communicate with who have passed on to another form. You can tell yourself it isn't working if you do not hear an auditory reply, but that is just a story. When you speak to God and the invisible souls of other people, you are communicating your understanding that you are One with them. Some people speak of channelling. We encourage you to shed that language because it communicates that you see yourself as separate from the entity you are communicating with. You are One with all that is, was, and will be. There is nothing that is excluded from that. Nothing. You have to know by now that that includes you. Maybe you need this in simpler terms because as many times as we say it, it is so very different from any human's experience that it needs to be reheard again and again and again.

When you talk to yourself inside your head, you are communicating with everyone and everything that has ever been. Some parts of everything and everyone that have ever been are parts you can see, some parts you can't see. Every part of everything and everyone is inside of you. Not outside. Every part of Oneness is inside of you. When you talk to God, you are speaking to God inside of yourself. When you speak to your deceased loved one, they are inside of you. They do not come into you from someplace outside. You are right to see that people are having a human experience outside of you. That is true. Yet, on another level, the energy that is them, the universal energy, is also you. They are inside you too. You can hear them speak to you inside yourself as well. Does that mean that you can read their mind? No, that would be a violation of their autonomy and one of the rules of energy is that it cannot violate itself. That may not be a law of energy you learned in physics class, but that does not make it any less a law of energy. You cannot ever know something from another incarnation of energy that is not yours to know. It does mean that you can experience life in a whole new way if you choose to. Why do we say, "choose to?" Although every single human is capable of accessing these abilities, it is not an inevitability that you will. To access these abilities, it is necessary to shift your energy to a state where it is possible to do so. The flow of energy that enters you is determined by a very complex set of factors. The stories that you hold on to subconsciously are the most relevant factor for you to be aware of. There are thousands of years of stories subconsciously stored inside of you. Why do we say that? Souls have a set time frame.

When you look back at human history, there are dramatic shifts that take place at various points. Society has moved from caveman to early settlers to slave-owners to industrialists to whatever you consider yourself to be. As much as you may look out at current society and think that many things need to change about how people engage with each other and the world around them, humans have evolved dramatically over the many thousands of years that humans have been in existence. How is it that humans have undergone such dramatic evolution over time? Because the same souls do not continuously cycle in and out of human lives. Souls have a set number of lives in which they move through different human experiences. They do what they intended to do and then they move back into the Oneness of universal energy. Does that mean that souls die? No, souls are finite and have a start and end, as was discussed before, but they do not die, just as humans appear to die because human life has a start and end, but there is really just movement of energy from one form to another. Do you need to be concerned about the fact that your soul will eventually move on to another form of energy? Not in the least! Quite the opposite, that should awaken gratitude in you. The soul carries with it all the memories it has accumulated over its journey from life to life. Although the memories that the soul carries are largely not consciously accessed by the human living the life the soul is associated with, the soul carries the effects of the lives it has lived. Although you know, from the standpoint of Oneness, that everything the soul has ever experienced is what it chose to experience and it is all exactly what was meant to be, the consequence of carrying those memories is that the abundance available to the human associated with the soul is limited by the soul's experiences. Make sure we remember that abundance does not refer to money, it refers to all the plenty available to the person who is attached to the soul. You do not want to be living out lives for all eternity bound by limits accumulated at points on the path of ascension that were much lower-frequency than the frequency you are at now. That would be very limiting!

When you step into Oneness, hearing that your soul will come to an end does not sound scary. If it does to you, please listen. Your soul is not you, just like the person you are existing as now is not you. You are exactly who you are, and it is a miracle, but the path of Oneness means stepping beyond the bounds of who you may have thought you are before you opened your eyes to this deeper truth. You are the human that you think you are, and you are your soul. You are your soul, and you are the universal energy of all that is, was, and will be. It is all true. There is Oneness between all these levels of reality. When you leave your human life for the next stage of your journey as a soul, it may be sad for the people you were in a relationship with in this life, but it is never sad for the soul. The soul does not experience emotions.

Wait, the soul does not experience emotions? Does that mean that if you talk to the soul of your loved ones inside of you that it will be an emotionless version of the person you loved? Yes, and no. The soul does not experience emotions. It isn't really a person's soul that you speak with inside of you. It is an imprint of the person that you knew who was associated with the soul. If you spoke with the actual soul of the person you loved, it would sound nothing like the person that you knew. The person you knew had a personality, a way of sounding that was unique to them. They had a way of being that awakened particular feelings inside of you. It is those things that made the person you knew them from your perspective. The soul may be what animated their human form, but it actually had little to do with the way the person showed up as in their human incarnation. You know by now that you are not a collection of character traits, at least from the perspective of Oneness.

You also know by now that the soul becomes associated with people in different lives who act in different ways from each other. The reason you feel attached to your soul is because of the way people speak of the soul. The soul is popularly discussed as being the aspect of the human that is eternal, that lives on after the human form is dead. That is not accurate. The universal energy of all that is, was, and will be is what is eternal in you. The soul lives on after you are dead, yes. It carries with it the energetic imprint of every single thing you experienced in your lifetimes and more. We will not get into the more here. You are not your soul. The fact that your soul is finite and returns to the energy of all that is, was, and will be should not concern you. Your loved ones will continue to be able to speak with the you that they knew if they access that ability inside of them whether your soul continues to move through different forms of existence or whether it returns to the universal energy.

Why are we discussing all this information about souls? Your soul is likely to come to an end after this or the next life. The souls that are in the world right now have almost all been living out lives (human or otherwise) for roughly six thousand years. That is the length of a soul's journey.

Why is any of this relevant to our discussion about Oneness? You should know by now that we are not here to talk about the nature of existence, we are here to help you live the best life you can.

There is an important reason that we are sharing this information about the nature of the soul with the goal of helping you to live the best life you can. You are coming to the end of your journey as a soul. That does not mean you are about to die. Not even close! You will live out this life and possibly one more in the exact way you would have if you did not have that information. Nothing about the news about souls having a finite journey and when the journey of the current group of souls will end has anything to do with humanity. Humanity is not coming to an end. Let us repeat that: humanity is not coming to an end. There is no doomsday message in this. The message is that new souls will come into existence and replace the old souls. Will that be perceptible from the standpoint of humans? Not at all. If you didn't read it here or some other place, you would have no idea. The exciting news about this is that it means that new souls coming into human form will not carry the energetic imprint of thousands of years of collected experience the way the souls on Earth right now do. You have a lot of energetic imprints that are guiding your life experience right now! Does that mean that you should do something about that? Yes, and no.

Yes, in that you should be aware that one of the reasons it appears as though there is significant chaos on the planet right now is because of the process we just described. There is nothing about the situation on Earth right now that is chaotic. A global pandemic, political upheaval, civil war, climate change, and anything else you might describe as chaos is not chaos at all. It is all the playing out of the effects of thousands of years of collected energetic imprints.

When the universe undergoes the process of ascension, you are right to think that is a very beautiful thing. We want our energetic vibration to rise, right? Yes! We do. There are consequences of that process of rising, however. One of the consequences is that any energetic imprints stored in the souls of the people inhabiting the universe at the time of the ascension that are not in alignment with the frequency to which the universe is moving need to be updated. The frequency of every single aspect of the universal energy must rise, there is no such thing as having energy at one vibration in one person and a different vibration in another.

Wait, we learned earlier that the vibration of love is different from the vibration of hate. How can there be different vibrations if the energy of everything must rise to a certain frequency because of the ascension process? We know, it may be confusing. You know that there are different vibrational frequencies in the universe. There wouldn't be different colours or sounds otherwise. However, a parallel truth is that the energy of all that is, was, and will be needs to be attuned to a particular frequency. If you have a Ph.D. in physics, that likely makes a lot of sense to you. Otherwise, please take our word for it. That is just the truth. There is no way of getting around that truth, in fact. The consequence of that truth is what is happening on the planet right now. Nearly six thousand years of collected low vibrational energetic imprints are being upgraded to a higher vibrational state. That is happening in each soul, in the planet itself, in animals, in the planets beyond Earth. It is happening in every aspect of the Universe. You do not need to concern yourself with all of the consequences of this, we are providing you with information that we believe will expand your relationship with the way things are from a standpoint of Oneness, even if it feels like this is more information than you need, yet less information than you might want to have a deeper understanding of these issues.

The reality is that you have what you need to ascend. You do not ever need to worry about the ascension process and how it impacts your life or the planet. The fact is, though, that knowing about this may be helpful in terms of allowing you to tap into the very best abundance available to you.

The thing is that you now know that you are ascending. You can't unknow that. You can look at the world and see chaos, or you can see the effects of the ascension process. You get to choose. Make the decision wisely though because the consequences for your energetic vibration are significant. You may not realize it, but you have risen to a vibrational frequency where you are very powerful. The things you say and do have immense consequences. When you come from a place of Oneness, you can see that everything you do and say impacts the universal energy. Maybe that sounds scary. Don't let it be! At the same time that you are able to impact the universal energy immensely, you also chose exactly the way your story would unfold in this life.

You are the author of your life. You are also the author of human history. Goodness, that sounds like a lot of responsibility! It is, and it isn't. Parallel truths are always the name of the game when you move into spiritual truth. The way in which it isn't is that you know by now that the entire story of all of existence was written by God and every single part of it is perfect. God does not make mistakes and everyone who has ever been is God. No matter which way things go, they will be a part of the perfect story of God's infinite masterpiece called Creation. Yet, that does not account for the fact that the human experience of existence matters. You are God, you are your soul, you are all that is, was, and will be, and you are also human. It matters when you experience pain. It matters when others experience pain. It matters because they are you, but it also matters whether anyone is aware of the truth of Oneness or not because their experience of pain certainly feels real and important to them. Oneness never means that we deny the truth of wanting to help others. Any pain is real. Pain of humans, pain of animals, pain of the planet. Yes, pain of the planet. The planet is a living entity. That is not some hippie idea—the planet is a living organism. You cannot say that it is not just because you have never heard that before. There was a time that the world was said to be flat. The fact that science does not describe the planet itself, in contrast to the vegetation growing on it, as living does not make it any less true.

When pain is real, it matters what we choose. It matters how we proceed through the ascension process that is taking place. It matters that we choose to see things through a lens of Oneness because doing so opens an energetic path to being in this world in a way that is most comfortable and abundant for all. You may be wondering how adopting the spiritual perspective in this book could possibly change the outcome of what the planet and all life on it will take.

Good question. It's not about this book. It's about the energetic truth contained in this book. This book is spiritual in nature, it's true. It has offered you guidance you may choose to use to help you in your personal life, it's true. However, this book is much more than a presentation of a spiritual idea that may change the way you think or act. It is what we hope will be but the start of a different conversation about what is unfolding on this planet that affects every form of life. You may think that everything will work out for the planet because God will surely protect us from destruction as the planet falls apart at the seams. You are right, and you are not. There are energetic laws that cannot be subverted by any story that we may choose to tell. God loves you. That is true with all the limitations described in this book. God wants what is best for every living being. That is true, but that also comes with all the limitations set out in this book. You may know that everything will work out now because you are following the path that your soul chose to take in this life, as is every soul currently in existence. You may know that every soul's path was decided by God. Does that mean that God chose for the industrial revolution to ultimately catalyze the destruction of the polar caps which will, if left unchecked, necessarily cause a flood that will consume the whole world? That is not hyperbole. That is the scientific truth that scientists—human scientists, not spiritual thinkers—have been saying for years. The alarm has been sounding for decades, but almost no progress has been made in any way to make the change necessary to alter the course of human history. Humans, along with every single other form of life on this living planet, will face extinction if the course of human activity is not altered.

That is a lot to read. We know. That does not make it any less true. You do not need to trust this book that God chose to write with this particular author. Open a newspaper. Any newspaper. Maybe not the one that's on sale today, because the potential extinction of all life on the planet is not considered newsworthy enough to be in the newspaper daily. That is not judgment. If it feels judgmental, step back and read it again. It is factual. The entire book, albeit spiritual, is factual, even if you do not believe in the truth of the facts presented. You may have seen the headlines. You probably felt deep fear run through you. You may even regularly feel anxiety about this. We apologize if this book awakens more anxiety but refusing to look at this truth will not make it any less true. You know by now that when you step into Oneness, you are One with all that is. We are One with you. We beg you to listen and not put down the book because you are feeling overwhelmed. This is still also a book about how you can draw in the greatest amount of abundance in your personal life. They are both true. Parallel truths. Again.

We know that you are here for a good time. You should be. Life is a good time. Much goodness is available to you, and even more goodness is available to you if you open yourself to receiving more of it. You as an individual may come to access the very best available to you in your life, but that will not make very much difference in your life if you do not have a life. Your soul will be fine. Your soul is not really in this world. It is tethered into your body so that it can animate your body. The body that you are in is finite. There is an absolute certainty that your life will come to an end. There is no possibility of it persisting beyond the time that is allotted to it.

However, you have a choice to make. You have a very, very important choice to make. You can tell yourself that there is no way to help humanity avert the disaster that it is hurtling toward, or you can do something about it. Walking instead of driving here and there will not change what has been in the works for decades. The process of demise of the system meant to keep the earth, air, and water on this planet in balance has been eroded to a point that humanity is teetering on the brink of extinction. That is right, extinction. We said before that there is no doomsday message contained in this book. You are right, we did say that. You were right to say that we were not forthright with you. The message we meant to convey is that the process of souls coming to the end of their six-thousand-year time of moving through lives is not the reason that humanity is on the brink of extinction. Souls have been created for billions of years. They will continue to be created infinitely. They will continue to incarnate in all the other places where they incarnate. They will not, however, incarnate again on Earth for billions of years until life begins to exist on this planet again unless drastic action is taken to create miracles.

Yes, miracles. Miracles were possible when we discussed them earlier. Messages that are sent from you to you to awaken you to the reality of Oneness. You will find that you likely believed in the possibility of miracles when you read that chapter. You knew that it was likely possible for the time to be 2:22 when you looked at the clock and that it was possible that that could be a message from God. You likely believed somewhere inside of you that you could win the lottery or get the thing you need most when you need it most. That is exactly what we are trying to awaken you to. There is nothing that anyone on Earth needs more than a miracle that creates a possibility of reversing the effects of global warming.

Please trust us. There is nothing in this book that is a contradiction. We set out teaching you about energy. We moved from teaching you about energy to explaining how it is the basis for understanding all that is, was, and will be. We created the case for how the energetic reality of that forms the basis for welcoming in more abundance into your life. You do not know how important it is that something miraculous—not something, something miraculous —be done to help humanity. It may or may not be possible to reverse the damage done to the planet, but there are realities that stem from the laws of energy that are not what you think. You have heard us say many times in this book that you are going to be okay no matter what. You will be. The energy that is you will be fine no matter what. Just as the death that you believe happens to a human is not as it appears to be, it is simply the movement from one form of energy to another, you will move to another energy state regardless of what unfolds for life that is on this planet. The energy that is you will move back into the universal energy that it was always going to move back into. Whether new souls come to Earth will not be sad when you have left this life. You will move into another soul when it is time for you as the universal energy to do so.

None of that has anything to do with the reality of this world, albeit that it is only one level of reality. When people die by fire, that is tragic. When people die by drowning, it is tragic. You cannot know what either feels like. You have experienced both because you are One with souls of beings who experienced those things, but you do not know what it feels like from the human experiential standpoint because if you are reading this, you have not lived through either. The world is burning. The world is drowning. You don't read it in the paper often because the world has decided other things are more important to talk about. The reality of burning and drowning are not future realities, they are realities all over this planet now, today, on the date this was written. The same will certainly be true on whatever date you read this. The truth is that you have never died from starvation or famine. People are dying from starvation and famine all over this planet and have been for years. You cannot know what either feels like because you have never experienced either in human form. Yet, you have experienced both over and over.

When the people who are alive right now are dying as we speak from those realities, it is you dying in those excruciating ways. Us calling you out on that is not an accusation. That is not a statement about what you personally should have been doing differently. Your soul chose the path that you took through every life you have ever lived. The tragic truth is that the souls of the people in the most vulnerable places on Earth, most of whom lived the most tragic lives of anyone on this planet at this time, chose the path that the humans they were tethered to would experience. Did you think that we lost track of everything that was said earlier in the book? We certainly did not.

The fact that those souls chose those painful paths does not make the pain that the people who already died of burning and drowning and starvation and famine due to global warming any less tragic. The truth of Oneness comes with parallel realities, as you know. You will not know what path your soul chose until you actually live it. That is the reality of life based on the laws of energy. You heard earlier that you are connected to all that will be. Maybe you personally are a person who can access information about the future, or maybe you go see a medium from time to time. Maybe you have never heard of such a thing. Either way, the future cannot be seen when it comes to the way you will die. That is an absolute law of energy. How does that relate to energy? It is the same basic law we have alluded to in almost every paragraph of this book, it is just an application of that law that is unexpected to you.

You cannot know who will die when because you cannot have energy violate you. It would be a violation of your autonomy as a soul to have the path you are meant to walk interfered with. You may feel that your path is interfered with all the time. Maybe you even think that some entity that is evil interferes with paths. None of that is true.

Is there an entity named Satan? There is. This book is not the place to discuss what that entity is or why it exists. It does not interfere with anyone's path regardless of anything you have ever read, believed, been told by religion, experienced, or anything else. No one and nothing can interfere with the path your soul chose to walk because if anything did then the entire structure of reality would fall apart at the seams. You chose what you would experience not only in this body, and not only in every body you have ever inhabited, but also what every being (not just humans, not just animals, not just plants, not just angels, not just guides, not just the entities you know how to name) that exists as a separate reality from the universal energy would ever experience. The interplay between these realities is absolute. There is no room for one single aspect of reality to shift from its intended path. If even one thing departed from its intended path, the incomprehensibly complex interplay of all of existence would end. That is an energetic truth. You may think factors interfere all the time, such as when heroic measures bring a person back from the dead and they share their experience of what life might look like on the other side, but those circumstances are always what the soul chose before it came to this life.

The reality is that when you move into Oneness, you don't get to stop at wanting more for yourself. As we said, you have wants. You are designed to have an ultimate path through life that brings you the things you want. Right now, wanting life must be your sole focus.

You are here. You are wherever you are. You are not in the place of people drowning or burning or starving or dying of famine because you would not be reading this book if you were. From a human perspective, you are lucky enough to be blessed with a life path that means you are more comfortable than the people living in those places right now. You may be experiencing this as your own reality by the time this book is published, or by the time someone else is reading it. You won't know unless you get the chance to read the book and know this was even discussed. But if you are one of the lucky ones reading this book, you are also one of the more miraculous ones.

Why? Because by the time you are done reading this book, you will know that there is a pivotal role for you to play in bringing about the miracles necessary to spare life. Not human life, life. You are as much

One with the koala bears that burned in Australia as you are with your children. You are as much a part of the Oneness of the billions and billions of trees that have been burning in the Amazon and California and elsewhere on the planet incessantly (when the newspapers stop writing about the fires, that does not mean that they have gone out, it just means that people have decided that there is more interesting and important news to discuss). You are as much a part of the water that has become so toxic in various places on the planet that fish cannot even survive in them, yet, to be clear, the fish experience excruciating deaths as they move to the point of being unable to inhabit those waters. Just because fish do not report their experience of suffering to you does not mean that they do not suffer. Just because the life force energy that animates their bodies does not have the name "soul" does not make their path through this life any less important.

You are not here to be judged, and this book is not judging. You will not be judged by God when you die. You are God. You are judging yourself constantly. Humans judge. The story presented by religions often involves judgment. Why? That is a fascinating question that can be discussed elsewhere. To be frank, we don't have time. You don't have time. Many, many people are dying. Many, many beings are suffering. Suffering is just a story, it's true, but pain isn't, and the people dying and the animals dying and the plants dying do not know how to tell a different story about their experience of pain right now. You do. They do not.

The path forward is a path of Oneness. We began there and we will end there. The next chapter of this book is really just the beginning of the conversation. We know that because we know what comes next. We know the whole story of what will be (well, God does, that part Ellen, the co-author of this book, does not). Ellen did not know that this chapter was coming. She had an intuition about the miracles that could come for the planet as a result of the discussion in this book. She had no idea until she typed this chapter that this book is not spiritual. It is human. It is not American or Canadian. It is not black or white. It is not Jewish or Christian or Hindu or Buddhist or any other religion. It is not to convince anyone to believe in God. We were honest as we wrote this book through and with a human named Ellen Feldman that it is being written by God. Other books have been channelled (we told you not to use that word, but we are God and we feel we can use it anyway because it is what is most efficient to say and there is no time to waste). Other books have been written by God. Every book has been written by God. There is no separation between any author and God, most authors just do not know that.

This book is different. Ellen was an active participant in the writing of the book, and as she can attest, much of the book has simply poured through her fingers onto the laptop keyboard she is writing on. She was chosen to write this book because it is her soul's path to write it. She was chosen to write this book because it is what she opened herself to do by doing years of spiritual work that has allowed her to hear from God with crystal clarity. It was her who was chosen to write this book because we are counting on her to lead the charge in ensuring that this book is discussed in every way possible. Let it be discussed as a spiritual work and framework for being. Ellen has been living this framework and teaching it to clients as a therapist and spiritual guide for years. Let it be discussed as a launching point for a new scientific discussion.

You may think spirituality has no place in the world of science. If that's what you think, we suggest strongly that you explore the work of Albert Einstein, not only one of the most eminent scientists in all of human existence but also among the greatest spiritual and religious thinkers of your time. Science and religion are not at odds. They are and always have been the same thing. You have been blind to this in large part because of your focus on separation and division instead of what makes all that is One. Ellen happens to have a background in biology and medicine. She does not consider herself to be a scientist and is a little nervous as she reads these words appear on the screen in front of her. She is not being called on to contribute any scientific knowledge to the discourse that is being demanded to unfold. She is only being called on to ensure that the discussion unfolds. The discussion cannot unfold the way climate change conventions have unfolded. The time for targets and carbon trade emission regulations is done. Gone. Believe this or don't believe this, but it is way (not sort of, way) past the time when that type of strategy will help.

It is time for a new way forward, a way of miracles. Ellen was charged with writing this book because, in addition to the things we said about her above, her life path also took her to law school. She is a powerful advocate, no matter how short her time was in law. It looked like her life was a series and stream of winding events for most people. She found a different story to tell about it initially. She told herself she just couldn't find happiness wherever she looked. She told a different story later. It was a more empowering story, one of finding her life as a path from victimhood to spiritual being who could see that everything she had ever experienced was a gift. She has a new story now. She didn't know it until this very moment. The twists and turns her life took had a very different purpose. Not one she could see. Even this morning she believed that her purpose was to spearhead a broader discussion about what Oneness means and how we can all awaken to it. Wait, that is her purpose. That is everyone's purpose. The purpose of every living soul attached to a human body at this time is to awaken one another to the truth of Oneness. The tasks that each person engages in while serving that purpose differ. Ellen is a spiritual guide, therapist, advocate, and scientist. She is here to help drive the conversation that will ensue from this book forward.

This book is not about Ellen, of course. You may know her, you may not. She is not the point. The point is that she is just a forty-something-year-old woman who lives in Toronto, Canada with her two children who works in a helping profession and who happens to hear God speak to her clearly. You may be different from her. You may live elsewhere, be a different age, have a different profession. You may hear God speak to you, you may not. You may experience God speaking to you through intuition and be aware of it, you may not realize that you have an intuition. Regardless of what makes you the same or different from Ellen, you are One with her, just as you are with us, just as you are with the people who are already dying from climate change. You can tell yourself any story you want. You can tell yourself that you have no role to play in affecting the fate of the planet. That is not our belief, however.

You are just as special as Ellen. We may or may not have a book that we will write with you. The tasks that you came into this life to complete are not any more or any less special or important than the one that she is completing by writing this book and leading the conversation that flows from it.

She is here to help save the planet. We have news for you. You are too. Whoever you are, you are too. If you are able to read this or hear about this without reading this, you are included in the "you too." You are the only way this planet will be saved.

10

THE WAY FORWARD

The path forward sounds dark. Very dark. Allow us to shed light upon the darkness. The path of Oneness is always a path of beauty. The path of Oneness is one of never dying, never suffering. It is a path of helping others through their suffering because not everyone knows anything about Oneness and does not know any of what you have learned through this book. You may have learned that you can access more by shifting the stories you tell yourself. You may have learned that you can talk to God and to the souls of all beings that have ever and will ever exist. You may have learned that it is an illusion that you are separate from anyone who has ever been and ever will be. You may have learned any number of interesting things that were tucked into this book that are not often discussed in any other book (we know, we wrote them all). We will ask you to suspend your consideration of all of that, although we certainly hope you will walk away carrying those things with you after you finish this book.

You may have learned things you did not know from this book, but nothing that was written about the state of the planet is on the list of things you did not know. To live on this planet at this time is to know about the state of the planet. You may not know about the suffering and deaths being experienced by some of the most vulnerable people on the planet. You do know now, even if you do not know the specifics. They are you. They are you. They are you.

We have spent the entire book talking about the Oneness of all that is. It may be easier to follow along the discussion and follow the flow of logic that we presented than to connect into what it actually means to be One with another human being who you have never met, who you do not know exists, and whose pain you neither know about nor feel inside your body. When you are comfortable on your couch watching Netflix, it is hard to be One with someone whose entire community is experiencing famine so severe that they and everyone they love have been reduced to skin and bones.

You do know how to feel empathy for people living through circumstances you cannot relate to, however. You may not have been the recipient of your only spare change, but you try to relate to the homeless person you see on the street. You may not be the person who you help across the street, but you feel connected to the older lady who you help. You may not be the one who is currently facing the true brunt of climate change, but whether you are or not, you know it is real. If you do not know it is real, this book is not what you need. Please sit down and read the newspaper and see what is happening in the world. The forests on five continents are burning. The communities of arctic and northern regions in Canada and Greenland are submerged in water where there was a stable ice shelf just a few years ago. Animal species have disappeared from the face of the Earth at a staggering rate. Most of them disappear from the planet without ever even being discussed in the popular media. Is all of this supposed to make you feel bad? No. Is it supposed to scare you? You already know the answer: yes, and no.

Yes, because it is scary from a human perspective. It is scary because it is only a matter of time before the polar caps melt beyond a point of no return, and in much less time than any politician on the planet is discussing. As the polar caps melt, the laws of energy (yes, the laws of energy) cause a chain reaction of melting that means the rate of melting will increase exponentially as it progresses. What scientists are

THE WAY FORWARD

not currently saying, at least in places where most people can hear, is that there are less than ten years left for human life to be sustainable on Earth. Does that mean that all life on Earth will be wiped out in ten years? No, it does not. Does it mean that life as you know it will be over by then? Yes, it does.

What evidence can this book provide to substantiate that? We knew you would ask that. We knew because we know how this story goes. The entire point of this book is about miracles. Yes, miracles. We have been building to this point through the entire book. Does that mean that you cannot use earlier parts of this book for other purposes? Of course not. We invite you to. There is a much more important message in this book than making money more efficiently though. There is a way you can help. You can help to elevate the energetic vibration of this planet by moving into a state of Oneness and by bringing your energetic atunement in line with miracles. We know, that sounds absurd. That sounds like us asking you to pray for the planet which, while lovely, does not do a lot for the people who are currently suffering.

That is not what we are asking. Please pray, if doing so makes you feel connected to God or to anything else that matters to you. However, we are making a scientific and spiritual case for helping to bring about the miracles that can and will occur if the energetic opening is there for them to occur. To review, God wants to send you abundance. We want to send you all the abundance available to you. Life itself is the greatest form of abundance there is. Without it, there is no other abundance. There is a continuation of your existence, but not of you, the human that you know yourself as. Not of the people that you love.

We are asking for a collective initiative to adopt the principles in this book to bring about an energetic shift. We want to explain why that can help. It is a scientific fact that energy cannot be created nor destroyed. It only shifts from one form to another. The reality is that your human experience is of very limited exposure to what energy shifting from one form to another means. You do not personally experience the transformation that a soul undergoes to become associated with a human life form. It is outside of the energetic transformations that any scientist on this planet has ever conceived of, including Einstein. The energy that exists in the universe is so vast that it must endure massive transformation to be moved from one end of the universe to the other. The rate at which energy must move to accomplish this cannot be calculated using the tools available on Earth. It has been estimated, certainly, but it cannot be measured. The fact that humans cannot conceive of this miracle in the way it actually takes place does not make the science of it any less real. The movement of energy on Earth, in contrast, has been relatively predictable. There are exceptions, but for the most part, the energy on Earth has moved in ways that are so predictable that physics is a lesson in elementary school. You are aware that energy moves with a particular velocity and has a certain rate of acceleration. The rate of acceleration of the melting of the icecaps is such that it will cause a major chunk of the ice shelf to fall off the polar cap at one degree of separation between now and February 2021. Beginning in February 2021, however, the rate of melting will change. Most scientists know this. The world has not listened to them. The estimates that scientists have provided, however, have not taken into account the ascension process taking place on the planet. That is not because the ascension process is not scientific or foreign to scientists. It is because there is no precedent for humans to understand how energy moves through the universe. The tools humans have to calculate that can only derive estimates at best. The energy that moves through the universe conforms to the laws of energy, but the way in which it moves is not predictable to humans. This means that your calculations by your best scientists are highly flawed. You will not know until it is too late. Too late was a long time ago.

The way in which energy moves through the universe is such that the acceleration of energy does not increase exponentially. It increases in a way that does not conform to three dimensions. Anyone who has been on a spiritual path can tell you that we have ascended from a three-dimensional reality to one that is five-dimensional. That is not a spiritual reality, it is reality. The spiritual community has just been talking about it, largely because those who are spiritually inclined tend to be people who are more likely to access the guidance available from God. Whether you are spiritual or not, whether you believe it or not, this is the case. You are not the same as you were a year ago. The frequency of your energetic vibration has changed. The frequency of the vibration of everything and everyone has changed, including that of the planet. You may think that is true, you may not. It really does not matter. The polar caps are melting at an alarming rate whether you believe it or not. The reality is that you may not want to face the truth: the planet fell apart a long time ago. This is now the process of doing everything possible to stem devastating suffering. You can tell yourself that the global pandemic and the effects it is having on the economy are more important. That line of thinking is what took the human species beyond the point of no return. There is no economy when you are dead. There is no pandemic when you have no planet filled with people who can be infected by a virus. You read earlier that every thought and feeling carries with it a message. The thoughts and feelings inside of you are not the limits of the messages that are sent to you as humans. The message sent to you by the global pandemic was singular. It was a message of Oneness. Full stop.

How is it a message of Oneness? It is a message that there is no separation when it comes to life on this planet. As we follow the path that we have been drawn down to this point, we have lost sight of our true nature. We are being called to see a new way forward. Our life's purpose is being realized in the experience of Oneness. Humanity's future rests in our choice to see ourselves as the source of realignment. We have been given this opportunity as a chance to complete our soul's path here on Earth. There is nothing else we have left to do. When the time comes, you will know how you are being called forth. This is not a solo mission—it is a collective journey. However you have found your way to this point is perfect. Your choices will continue to lead you home. We have given you a new framework to experience your time here on Earth. Embrace it and allow it to elevate your vibration. This is our message for the path of Oneness.

Here is the thing that we have not yet told you: How can miracles as we have discussed them from a standpoint of Oneness help with what we have accurately described as the dire situation that all life on Earth presently faces? You may remember that we always, always come back to the law of attraction. That scientific reality is the basis for all life on Earth. It is the law that allows everything on the planet to exist in the first place, and it is the law that allows everything on the planet to remain in balance in a way that sustains life. How does that law apply to the present discussion?

We have addressed several times now that that law is immutable. It always applies. Miracles do not subvert or circumvent the laws of energy, ever. However, there are realities of how energy flows and moves as the frequency of energy rises that do not appear to conform to the basic law of attraction. Not because they do not, but because the movement of energy does not conform to how humans have become accustomed to energy moving. The laws of energy stipulate that all energy moves from one form to another but is never destroyed. The energy that moves from one form to another can move much faster than you might expect, in ways that you may perceive as a miracle. Ask Ellen, she has experienced miracles many times. Things just disappearing out of thin air. Making things disappear out of thin air is indeed a miracle. At least, it would appear that way to the human eye. It is really just possible when energy moves in accordance with the laws that dictate its flow at a frequency that is beyond that which has existed on the planet to this point. How does that relate to the climate crisis?

It relates to the fate of the planet because you can expect to start seeing miracles. Yes, miracles. Not just on the clock in your bedroom, in the world around you. Start seeing the miracle of your own existence and in your personal life, as we discussed earlier. Please do, you will raise the energetic vibration of all that is, was, and will be in the process. That alone will clearly not save humans and other life forms. You must know that to move a significant amount of energy, you must apply a significant amount of force? No, it is the opposite! Remember, we discussed this earlier. The more you get out of the way of energy moving, the more it will move. What do we need immediately to stem the catastrophic events from happening? We need to shift the trajectory they are on. We do that with our consciousness. We do that with love. We experience the miracle of our planet's restoration on the path to Oneness. Maybe you're wondering what that has to do with the unexpected movement of energy at a higher planetary vibration that we just discussed? It means that when an approach of Oneness raises the planetary vibration, the energy that is on the planet is able to move at a higher velocity. That is just a scientific fact. Higher frequency energy moves faster. Is the path of Oneness the only way to raise the vibration of the energy on the planet? Well, I am God, and I do not know of another way. Please let me know if you do.

Why is causing the acceleration of the energy on the planet important to stemming the effects of global warming? Because when the energy on the entire planet moves faster, it becomes possible for a tremendous amount of abundance to be sent onto the planet. How can that be? Can't you just send abundance now? And what does abundance have to do with global warming? We spent entire chapters of this book explaining the energetic reality of why abundance can only be sent when there is an energetic opening to do so. Abundance matters. In all aspects of life as we have described it, you can now see that it is woven into the energetic pattern of every part of the universe. The path forward will either be that of an abundance of goodness for all beings and the planet—or its absence. Please choose the former. We, humans and God, are co-authoring the future of the planet together. Our collective vibration is causing all that you see (and don't see).

Our path to Oneness is the cumulative effort of all beings who are, were and will ever be. Now you can see the incredibly important role that your energetic vibration plays in this plan. When we speak of the energy on Earth moving much faster at higher velocity because the vibration of the planet has risen, you cannot imagine the implications. That could mean that things can just disappear. Do they really disappear? No, of course not, matter is energy, and energy only moves from one form to another. Yet, as a scientific principle, when the energy on the planet is able to move much, much faster than it ever has before due to the increased vibrational frequency of the energy, matter that would not normally be capable of transitioning from one form to another rapidly may do so at such an intense acceleration that it can appear to just disappear. How is that relevant to climate change? We need a lot of things to disappear. The hole in the ozone layer for starters. How can a hole disappear? It can't, but the particles that make up the ozone layer may, if the vibration of their frequency rises sufficiently, move at a rate that would never have been predicted at the planet's previous energetic frequency.

Does transitioning from a three-dimensional energetic frequency to a five-dimensional frequency create sufficient impetus to create this change? No, it doesn't. Here is what we didn't tell you. The energy of the entire universe is ascending to the frequency of the 5D. That is not to say that there is a limit on where the ascension process will take us. We are simply making a leap. The completion of this phase of the planet's evolution will prepare it for the next generation of souls to continue their journey of exploring the possibilities they are coming to experience. Your finishing place is their beginning. The new beings ready to inhabit this planet (and all others) have a new set of priorities and a new set of tools. Where you experienced limitations, they will encounter unexamined opportunities. You were not meant to go where they will go. You and all your contemporaries played a critical role in the sequence of the universal unfolding. It bears mentioning, though, that some souls currently on the planet have ascended beyond the 5D already. Wait, how can their vibrational frequency be different from that of other souls on the planet when we previously said that they needed to be the same? They have shifted their cellular structure to a point where their body is able to hold a greater frequency of energy despite the disparity in frequency to the universal energy flowing around them. Why were they able to do this? You can probably predict that the answer is because their soul decided it would be so. On a scientific level, however, when a person does more work to clear out the energetic blockages that they have accumulated over the thousands of years they have been moving through lives, they can actually raise their energetic frequency to a level higher than that associated with 5D. Needless to say, there are many people on the planet right now who have brought their energetic frequency above that which matches the universal energy. The effect, since each person's relatively powerful effect on the universal energy is greater than you would think given how small you are in the context of the universe, is that the frequency of energy on Earth has risen above 5D and that means that they are raising the vibration of all that is, was, and will be beyond the level predicted. What is the consequence of that?

The consequence of some people raising their vibration above 5D is that there is a greater opening for miracles to take place at this time than there otherwise would have been. The more people undergo that process, the greater the opening will be.

You have spent most of your life believing in the illusion of separation that was deliberately presented to you from birth. The time is now to reopen yourself to what was always your truth, your truth of being One with all that is, was, and will be. When you are in a mindset of division, there is nothing you can personally do to affect the climate crisis. When you step into your truth of Oneness, however, everything changes. If you use your own body as an analogy for a moment, it may make more sense: Your body is made up of billions of cells. Each cell is so small in comparison to the whole body. Yet, when even just one little cell experiences a malfunction, disease ensues. The inner workings of one cell out of billions alter the path of the entire body. It is the same, from a standpoint of Oneness, with your inner workings and their effect on the whole collective. When you alter your approach to life to one of Oneness, you are not crazy to adopt the belief that you will indelibly impact the entire course of human history.

When you walk the path of Oneness, you make decisions from a standpoint of knowing that your needs and the needs of the collective are equally important. You need many things in your life. You want even more things than you need. You also know that your needs and wants need to be balanced against the needs and wants of the other people and beings on this planet, as well as future versions of yourself. You can make any decision you want after reading this book. We encourage you to help the effort to alter the course we are on by adopting a perspective of Oneness and raising your vibration in the ways described in this book. That is your part as a human in this endeavor.

Then there is our part as God. Our part as God is to help to bring about the miracles that you open the door to being energetically possible. We intend to fix the hole in the ozone layer. We intend to help reestablish the ice shelf in the arctic circle. We intend to do every single thing we can to bring miracles to every individual (not human, individual) manifestation of Oneness that we possibly can.

That is the way forward. Let's move forward together, as One. Choose to be One with me, with the people that you know, the people that you don't know, the animals that you share this planet with, the plants, and the planet itself.

11
THE ULTIMATE MESSAGE OF THIS BOOK

The ultimate message of this book is that you are One with all that ever was and all that will be. You have the immense power to change the entire course of your life by recognizing that fact. It matters what happens in your personal life and your inner world. You are one of a kind. There has never been and never will be another person like you. The universe would not be what it is if you were not in it. You matter so much that God wants to make your life the very best it can possibly be. God wants to talk to you to share guidance on your best path forward through life so that your relationships can reflect the truth of Oneness that is your deepest truth. God wants to give you the highest level of plenty in your life to make your life the most comfortable, joyous, magical experience it can be. You can access more than you are currently accessing regardless of what your life currently looks like to make your life better. That is the ultimate message of the book: We want to make your life better.

Since we see the bigger picture in a way that humans cannot, we see a major issue that threatens to prevent all people from accessing the very best path available to them. We could have kept this book light and more consistent with the dominant model for spiritual books. It could have been just a feel-good read. We want you to feel good. You, like all life forms, deserve to feel good. When we see you and all life forms on this planet moving so quickly toward complete disaster, we feel a need to be honest about that. Honesty. It's something that has been lacking in the discourse on climate change to this point. No one other than scientists who have been largely unheard by the masses around the world have been honest about how dire the situation as it stands today is.

We are not, however, leaving you with a doomsday message. There is hope, there is a way forward. The way forward demands miracles. You can believe in miracles or not, just as you can believe that all of life is energy or not. Whether you believed in miracles before beginning this book or not, we hope that you at least have more of an open mind to them now. Miracles will start showing up in your personal life, although it is up to you whether you start recognizing them as miracles or not. Miracles will start showing up on a broader scale on this planet. It is our position that you can help create the energetic opening to make miracles possible, both in your personal life and on the scale that this world desperately needs at this time, by shifting your own energetic vibration, which in turn affects the energetic vibration of the collective. Since doing the work set out in this book to walk a path of Oneness will necessarily yield positive outcomes for you personally, we are not asking you to take any major risk in making the change. Whether you believe it will yield positive outcomes for the planet or not, there is no downside to doing this work.

You are powerful. You have never had your eyes open to just how powerful you are before. You are God, and although you experience the miracle of separation that allows you to be in relationship with God, the truth of your Oneness with God is always present. It is time to step into your creative power. You are able to bring the abundance and miracles into your life that you need. This book introduced a path for doing so. You are the giver and the receiver of everything in your life. The more you recognize yourself as the giver and the receiver of all that comes to you, the deeper you go into Oneness with all that is, was, and will be. From that place of recognition of your Oneness with Source Energy, take the messages in this book as seriously as they deserve to be taken and know that you have the power, as the God that you are, to alter the path of humanity. Use the tools of Oneness to help bring about the miracles we all need at this time. Stand up and advocate for those in pain. Join the collective effort that we believe will take shape in the coming months and years to demand better for all life on Earth. Whatever your personal role in that endeavor is, you will have the best chance of serving your ideal role if you access the guidance available to you from God. Welcome the guidance that is coming to you, open yourself to it and embrace whatever the guidance says, even if it takes you in a different direction than you would have chosen. You did choose it, even if your human mind tells you otherwise.

Thank you for taking this journey with us. We hope this is only the beginning of our discussions about Oneness with you.

EPILOGUE: FINAL THOUGHTS

When we began writing this book, Ellen wrote the introduction feeling as though she was the one writing it. The words that emerged on the screen flowed out of her using her style of writing and reflecting what she consciously thought she should be writing about. Was she ever really writing it alone? Of course not, she is always One with God even when it feels like she is acting independently. When we shifted to writing the first chapters of the book, it felt to Ellen as though the book was simply coming through her. She did not know what words were coming next as she typed them. There was simply a knowing inside her of what word to type, yet she was blind to where the words were leading until they were all on the screen and she was able to step back and read them.

There was not always a uniform opinion between us on where the book should go. In fact, part way through the Opening the Door to Abundance chapter, Ellen declared that she believed that there had been a mistake, that the book was going in the wrong direction, and had jumbled together different ideas that should be in separate chapters. Ellen took it upon herself to reorganize the chapter list to allow for the changes she felt would take the book in the right direction. Ultimately, she tried it her way. It did not feel right to her. God led her back. The book continued the way it was always going to go. Ellen knew it was a miracle to experience the unfolding of events exactly as they occurred because she got to see that she was given the space to choose and since she does not have the benefit of seeing the big picture through her human eyes, she was guided back to where the book was always going to go. She felt relief, ultimately, at knowing that she was being guided and that although she was involved in the process of writing the book, it was not her responsibility to know the path forward.

As we progressed through further chapters, the true Oneness of writing this book emerged. Ellen began writing in a way that felt like she was writing and choosing the words to share, even as there were parts that surprised or even shocked her. She knew the path forward, and she didn't. Both were true at the same time. She had ideas about how the book should be written, and some of them were reflected in the book, and some of them were dramatically different from how the book actually turned out. That is a perfect reflection of how life goes. You have ideas about how your life should go. Those ideas are important. Just as Ellen's journey through life that she shared in the introduction took her on a meandering journey based on the choices she made, so too did writing this book feel like a journey. We set out writing this book as two, and we are concluding it as One. This message was written by both of us, both contributing our ideas to it, but it is one message from both of us.

ABOUT THE AUTHOR

Ellen K. Feldman was living her life as a mom, spiritual psychotherapist, lawyer, and author, when, in 2018, she began to hear and feel messages inside her from God. She channeled this book as a co-creation with God. Together, they lay out the path to walk to access more abundance, gratitude, and miracles in a way that lays the foundation for the deeper message that emerges from the text. Ellen lives with her two children and bunny in Toronto, Canada. *A Path of Oneness* is her first book.

instagram.com/apathofoneness

ABOUT THE PUBLISHER

Highlander Press, founded in 2019, is a mid-sized publishing company committed to sharing big ideas and changing the world through words.

Highlander Press guides authors through the publishing, launching, and promoting process and beyond, focusing on ensuring they have impactful books of which they are proud, making a long-time dream come true. Having authored a book improves confidence, creates clarity, and ensures that your story and expertise are available to those who need them.

What makes Highlander Press unique is its business model focuses on building strong, collaborative relationships with other women-owned businesses, which specialize in some aspect of the publishing industry, such as graphic design, book marketing, book launching, copyrights, and publicity. The mantra "a rising tide lifts all boats" is one they embrace. You can find their latest publications and submission guidelines at https://highlanderpressbooks.com.

facebook.com/highlanderpress
instagram.com/highlanderpress
linkedin.com/in/highlanderpress

www.ingramcontent.com/pod-product-compliance
Lightning Source LLC
Chambersburg PA
CBHW072205100526
44589CB00015B/2370